Cello Chords

By

Bryan Wilson

Photo: Sydney Perlow

Published by

Bryan Wilson

1053 Oakland Court

Teaneck, NJ, 07666

www.bryanwilsoncello.com

ISBN 978-0-9838767-0-

Table of Contents

Acknowledgements

This book would not have been possible without the many cello teachers I have had the honor of studying with. In the order that I studied with them: Elizabeth Kalfayan, Tómas Ulrich, Barbara Mallow, and especially Erika Duke-Kirkpatrick. Thank you to my composition teacher, Art Jarvinen, for everything you gave me, I miss you. Thanks to Ulrich Krieger and Rohan de Saram for their helpful suggestions on this book.

I'd like to thank my parents, Paul and Sydney, for always being so supportive and for paying for my musical education (and therapy appointments). To my brother, grandparents, cousins, aunts, and uncles, I love you guys and thank you for putting up with me. To my cousin, Ben Bolin, you did an amazing job designing the cover of this book. I can't thank you enough.

To Anna Varnon-Grier, thank you for helping me grow as a comedian and human being, you have the biggest heart in the world. To everyone I love at CalArts, thank you for being part of my life. You guys are wonderful.

I want to thank myself for putting the time and energy into doing something I believe in. You can be a real jerk off sometimes, Bryan, but you've got a good heart.

Lastly, thank YOU for purchasing this book. If I can help one other person out there make great music on the cello, this book was worth it.

If not, I think I'll become an accountant.

Author's Note

I started writing this book during the summer of 2008, when I was working as a lifeguard at a pool in New Jersey. I have to admit, I wasn't a stellar employee, seeing as I hated the job with a passion and spent most of my working hours writing down cello chords, instead of ensuring the safety of dozens of young children.

Before you get angry with me for endangering the lives of our precious youth, I'll have you know that no one was hurt on my watch...or lack there of.

Thankfully, that was the last summer I was ever a lifeguard. Had I continued working that job, I'm sure I would have dozed off at some point, some kid would have drowned, and I'd be writing this book in Rahway State Penitentiary right now.

But I'm not in jail yet, which is great.

In all seriousness, I got the idea for this book at the New Directions Cello Festival in June 2008. A fellow cellist inspired me with his unique approach to the instrument and his deep interest in chords. He told me he liked to figure out as many ways to play the same chord on the cello as he possibly could.

We parted ways after the 3-day festival and I thought to myself, "Why don't I try figuring out all the ways to play a C chord on the cello?" After discovering only a couple of new chords, I quickly realized how boring a task this was. I decided to look online to see if anyone had written a book that had already done the work for me.

There was none.

I couldn't believe it. If I wanted to explore all different types of chords on the cello, I'd have to do the work for myself. This wasn't welcome news to someone who grew up in a cushy middle class suburb and was used to everything being handed to him gift-wrapped, with a pretty lime green bow on top.

But I decided I wanted to do it. So I put in the countless hours of work it took to produce this book so that you never, ever have to subject yourself to such grueling torture.

2

Trust me, this book was about as interesting to write as it is being stuck behind that woman in line at the grocery store, who forces you into an endless one sided blabathon about her 15 cats, and who doesn't seem to realize that your facial expression and body language could only be interpreted by any rational human being as crystal clear signals of extreme boredom.

Nevertheless, writing this book was undoubtedly worth it. The cello is an instrument with more musical possibilities than most people give it credit for. Though I grew up playing classical music, I was always interested in more contemporary styles, such as rock, pop, electronic music, and improvisation. Why couldn't the cello be used in all of these situations?

The bottom line is that the cello CAN do all these things and more. I think this book opens up a lot of possibilities for cellists looking to go beyond the traditional classical repertoire. Say you find yourself in a rock band and you need to play the chords for the verse. Open up this book and you'll find plenty of fresh ways to make that chord progression shine in your song.

Say you're improvising and looking for harmonies to take your improvisations to new places. There are plenty of chords in this book that could serve as the basis for a whole improvisation.

The possibilities are endless. The point of this book is to help cellists play music in the 21st century and to become more comfortable using the cello as a harmonic instrument.

Let this book help you in anyway you see fit.

Write new compositions with it.

Use it to play in unconventional musical settings.

But most importantly, let it be a part of your journey to cultivate a creative voice on the instrument.

How to Use this Book

Chord Types

The book covers all 12 keys and each key has 11 chord types.   The following are the chord types in the order they appear in each key:

1) Major = C = C - E - G

2) Major 7th = $C^{\Delta 7}$ = C - E - G - B

3) Dominant 7th = C^{7} = C - E - G - Bb

4) Augmented = $C+$ = C - E - G#

5) Augmented Major 7th = $C+^{\Delta}$ = C - E - G# - B

6) Minor = $C-$ = C - Eb - G

7) Minor 7th = $C-^{7}$ = C – Eb - G - Bb

8) Minor Major 7th = $C-^{\Delta}$ = C - Eb - G - B

9) Half-Diminished 7th = $C^{\varnothing 7}$ = C - Eb - Gb - Bb

10)   Diminished = C^{0} = C - Eb - Gb

11)   Fully Diminished 7th = C^{07} = C - Eb - Gb – Bbb

Notation (refer to videos demonstrating these techniques at www.bryanwilsoncello.com)

9th

The chord has an added ninth in addition to the root.

LS (Lift and Strum)

A lift and strum chord is executed by first fingering and plucking the bottommost note of the chord. Immediately afterwards, lift the finger for this note while fingering the other notes of the chord, strumming from low notes to high notes. The purpose of this is to reduce the strain on your hand, as well as to allow for better resonation of the upper three strings.

Pull

A pull chord is executed by plucking the bottommost note of a chord with the indicated finger. Strum the subsequent notes as you pull that finger **over** the other strings and place it in the same position on the "A" string, the "D" string (where noted), or both the "D" and "A" strings (where noted). The number after the word, "Pull," indicates what finger should be pulled. Because the hand position has to be altered during mid-chord, the pull chord has to be arpeggiated. This process can be reversed by starting on the "A" string and strumming from the top down.

> Note: In some cases, the *two* bottommost notes are to be played with the indicated finger. In these cases, pluck these two notes with the indicated finger, and then follow the same procedure as a regular pull chord.

Pluck

A pluck chord involves picking up certain strings and leaving others stationary. To perform a pluck chord, finger the notes of the chord on the correct strings, and pluck only those strings with the right hand.

Pluck Pull

Perform this type of chord by plucking the bottommost note of the chord first, then plucking the second highest note while pulling the indicated finger across the cello to the A string. Finally, place the indicated finger on the A string and pluck. The resulting chord will be arpeggiated.

LP (Lift and Pluck)

To Lift and Pluck, first pluck the bottommost note of the chord and then lift that finger. Then finger the top two notes of the chord and pluck them individually. The resulting chord will be arpeggiated.

Pizzicato

The chords in this book should be played pizzicato. If you are so inclined to try them with the bow, go ahead, but the book is not really designed for bowing.

Finger Numbers

Each chord has suggested fingerings next to each note in the chord. The fingerings go as follows:

 0 = Open string

 1 = Index finger

 2 = Middle finger

 3 = Ring finger

 4 = Pinky

 ♀ = Thumb

Note: Chords that have these intervals; unison, major second, or minor second will have 2 finger numbers that are written next to each other, instead of on top of one another. In these cases, the first finger number applies to the left note of the interval and the second finger number applies to the right note of the interval.

String Numbers

Some chords have string numbers next to each finger.

The string numbers are as follows:

 I = A string

 II = D string

 III = G string

 IV = C string

Note: String numbers are only used when I feel they help to clarify how and where to play the chord.

Order of Keys

The keys are arranged in circle of fifths order, starting with C and going clockwise. The order is as follows:

C – G – D – A – E – B – F# - Db – Ab – Eb – Bb – F

The enharmonically equivalent keys, Cb, Gb, and C# are not listed in the book since they are the same exact chords as B, F#, and Db respectively.

Chord Order

The chord order for each specific tonality is as follows:

1. Root Position: Ex. D7 = D in the bass
2. First Inversion: Ex. D7 = F# in the bass
3. Second Inversion: Ex. D7 = A in the bass
4. Third Inversion: Ex. D7 = C in the bass

Chords with the same inversion are listed in the order of difficulty, starting with the easiest and ending with the hardest. For example, the easiest third inversion D7 chord will be the first D7 chord listed with a C in the bass, while the hardest third inversion D7 chord will be the last chord listed with a C in the bass. The level of difficulty is relative only to the specific inversion of the chord. This means that the last root position chord will most likely be more difficult than, say, the first second inversion chord, even though the root position chord comes first in the list.

Note: A chord's difficulty will differ from one cellist to another due to hand size, strength, skill level, etc. Nevertheless, I feel this ordering gives, at the very least, a good approximation of difficulty.

Fingerings

Because every cellist's hand is different in terms of size, flexibility, and strength, the fingerings I listed are suggestions. If you find fingerings that work better for your hand, by all means, use the one that feels best.

Bonus Section

This section covers extended chords including power chords, 9ths, 11ths, 13ths, sus chords, and slash chords. This is by no means an exhaustive list, but more of an introduction to even more chordal possibilities on the cello.

> Note: The * symbol denotes that these chords lack the third, thus making them a bit ambiguous in terms of function.

Demonstrational Videos and Questions

For demonstrational videos on how to use Cello Chords, please visit www.bryanwilsoncello.com. In these videos, I demonstrate how to effectively play the chords in this book, so you can easily apply it to your own music making.

For questions or comments about this book please contact me at bryan@bryanwilsoncello.com

Musical Examples

The following musical examples demonstrate one of the many uses of Cello Chords: adding harmonies to a preexisting melody. I chose two recognizable folk songs: House of the Rising Sun and Sloop John B.

House of the Rising Sun

Traditional
Arranged by Bryan Wilson

Sloop John B

Traditional
Arranged by Bryan Wilson

10

!!!!CAUTION!!!!

To Cellists: This book can make your hand <u>VERY TIRED, VERY QUICKLY</u>. If you feel even the slightest bit of discomfort, STOP PLAYING! The last thing I want is for anyone to get hurt! Please, please, please, just use common sense and DO NOT push yourself to the point of pain! Not being able to play cello because you are injured is not fun. (Trust me, last time I got injured playing the cello, I had to become a comedian-cellist...Please for your own sake, don't go down that road.)

To Composers: This book has some very difficult and awkward chord positions for cellists. DO NOT expect them to be able to play some of these chords very fast or extremely gracefully. Consult a cellist if you are writing a piece and using this book as a reference, so you don't end up writing something that is unplayable.

C

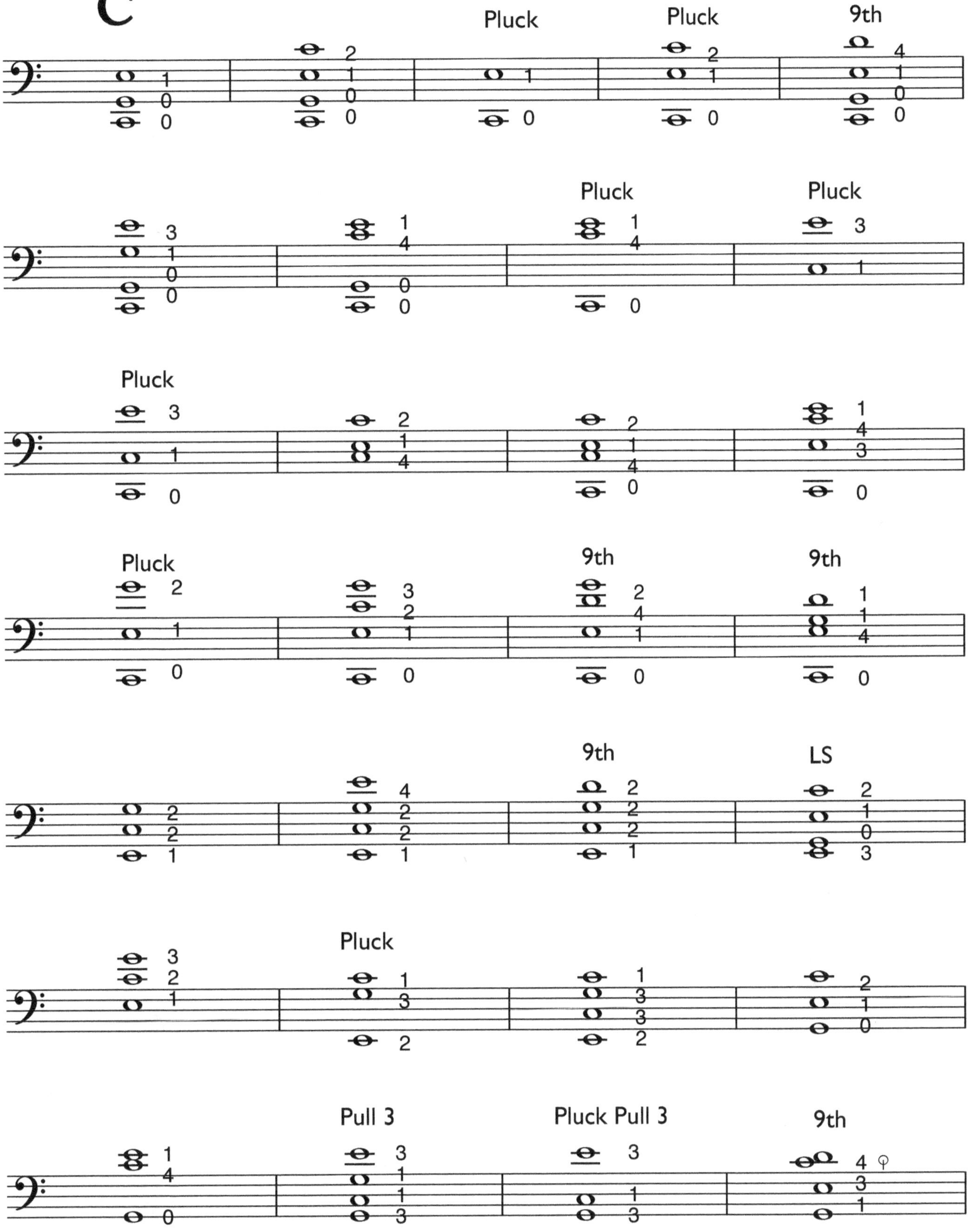
Pluck
Pluck
9th
Pluck
Pluck
Pluck
Pluck
9th
9th
9th
LS
Pluck
Pull 3
Pluck Pull 3
9th

C△7

C7

13

C+

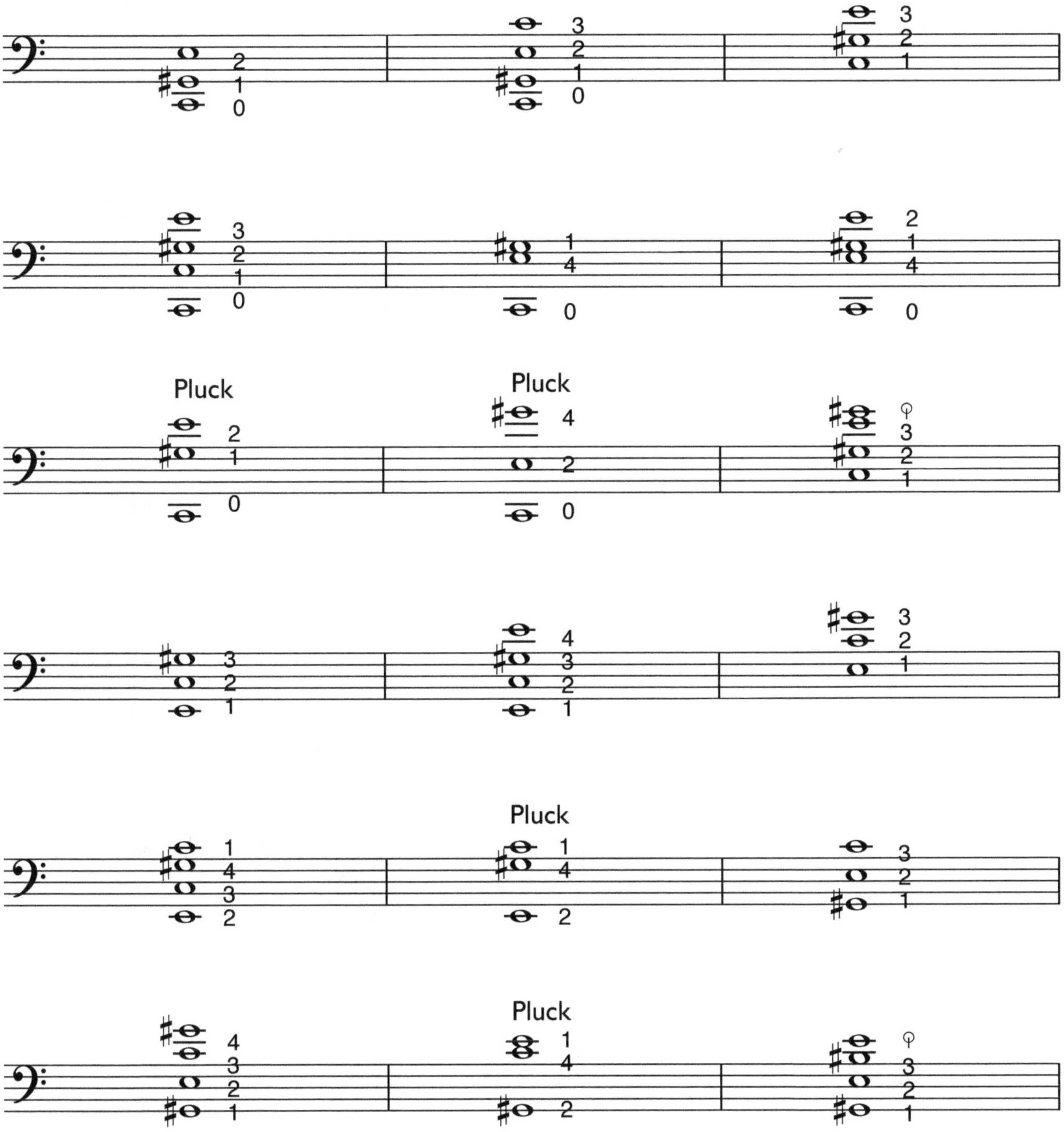

C+Δ

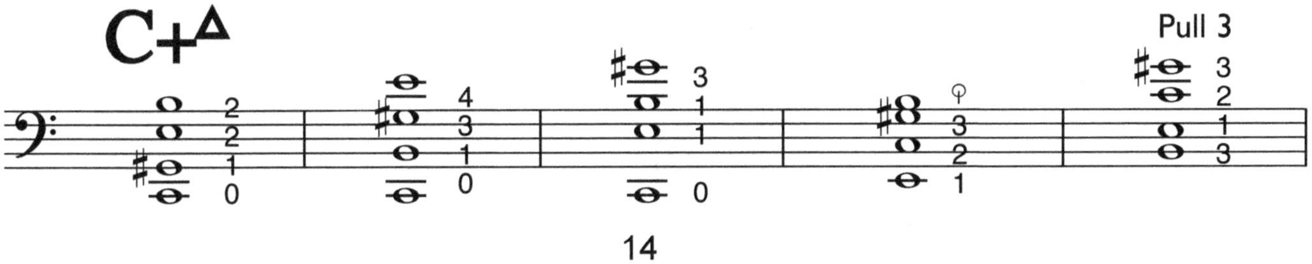

15

C-7

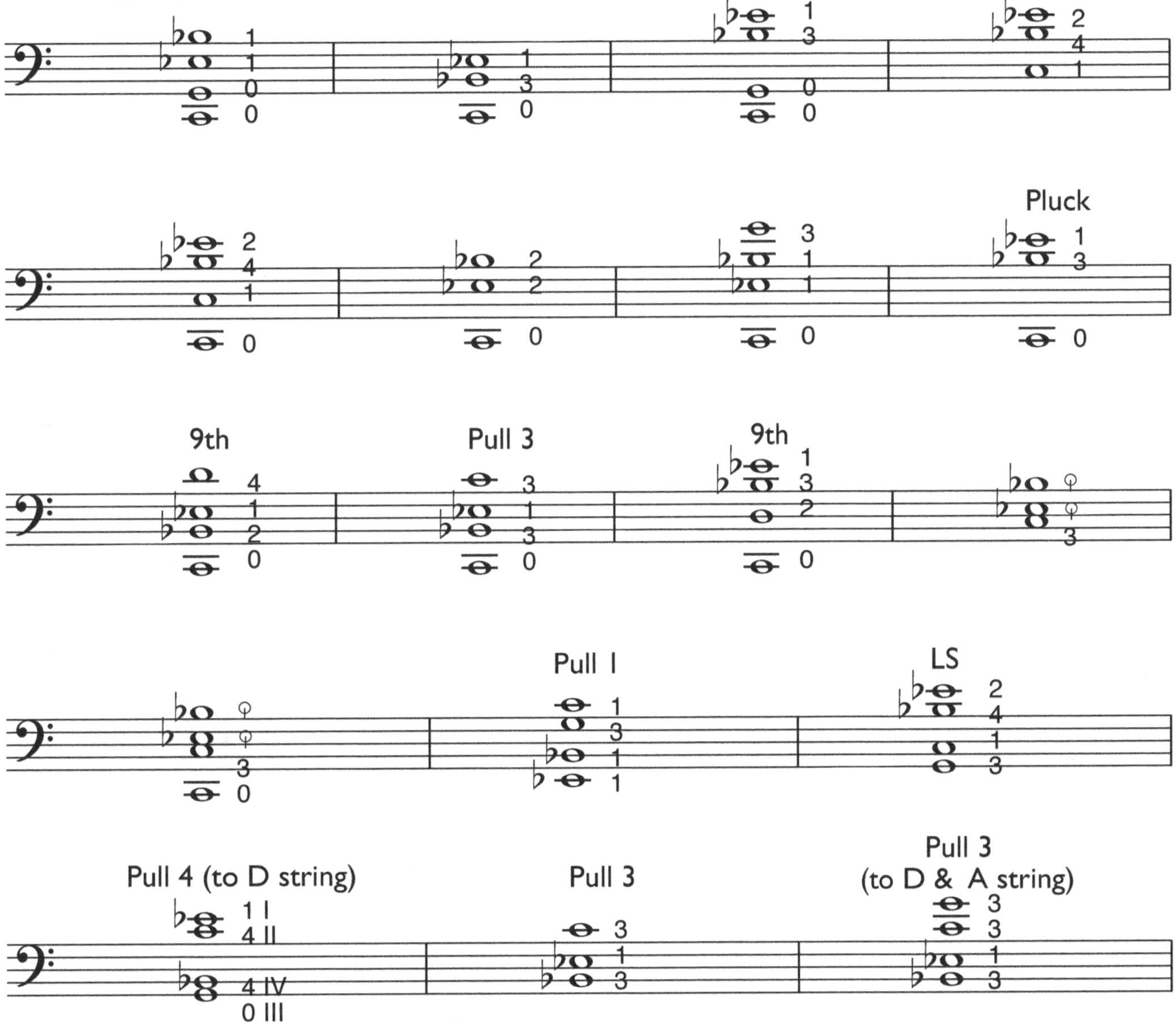
Pluck
9th
Pull 3
9th
Pull I
LS
Pull 4 (to D string)
Pull 3
Pull 3
(to D & A string)

C-Δ

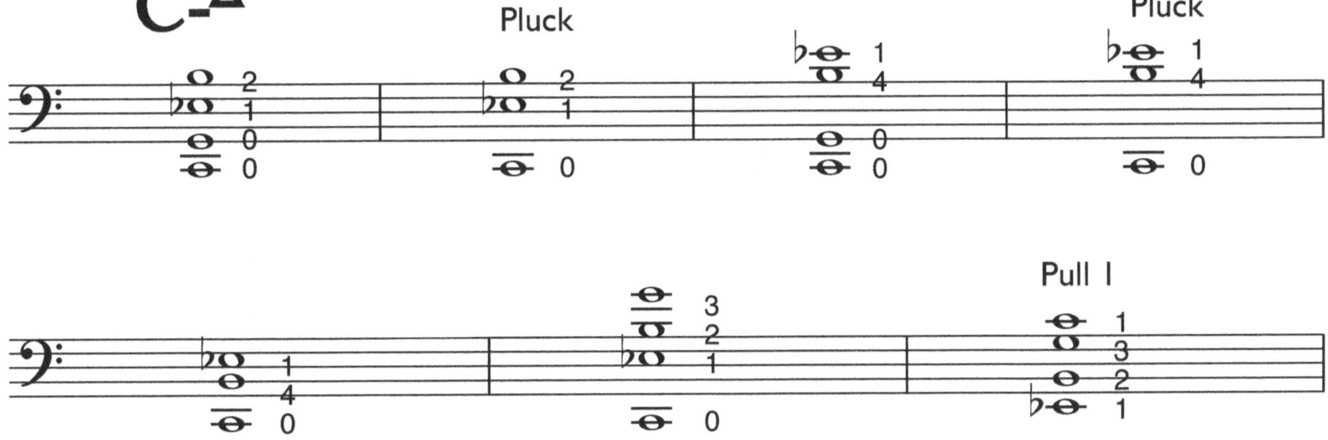
Pluck
Pluck
Pull I

Cø7

Pull 3 (to D string)

C°

Pluck

Pluck

Pull 1

Pluck Pull 2

C°7

Pull 2

Pull 2

Pull 2

17

G

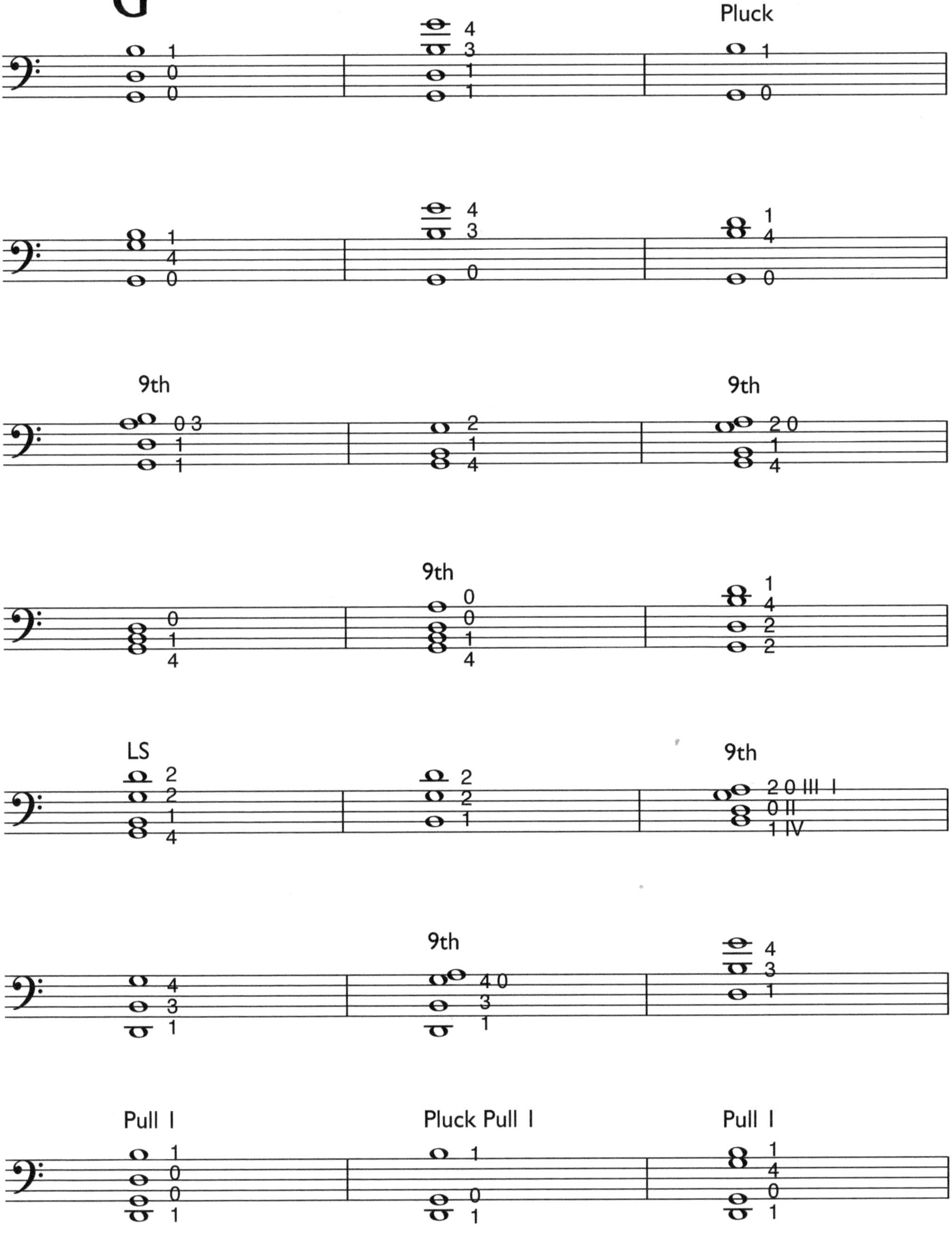
Pluck
9th
9th
9th
LS
9th
2 0 III I
0 II
1 IV
9th
Pull I
Pluck Pull I
Pull I

G$^{\Delta}$7

9th
LS
9th
Pull 1
9th
9th

G7

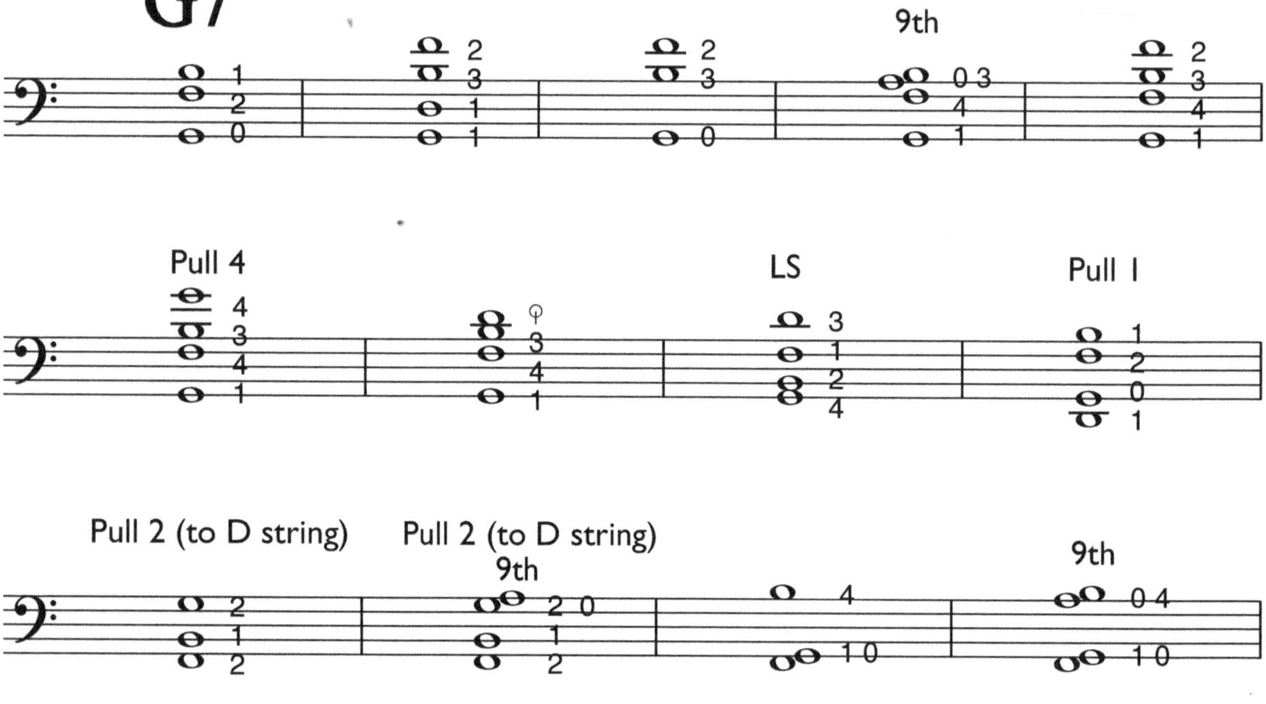
9th
Pull 4
LS
Pull 1
Pull 2 (to D string)
Pull 2 (to D string)
9th
9th

20

G-

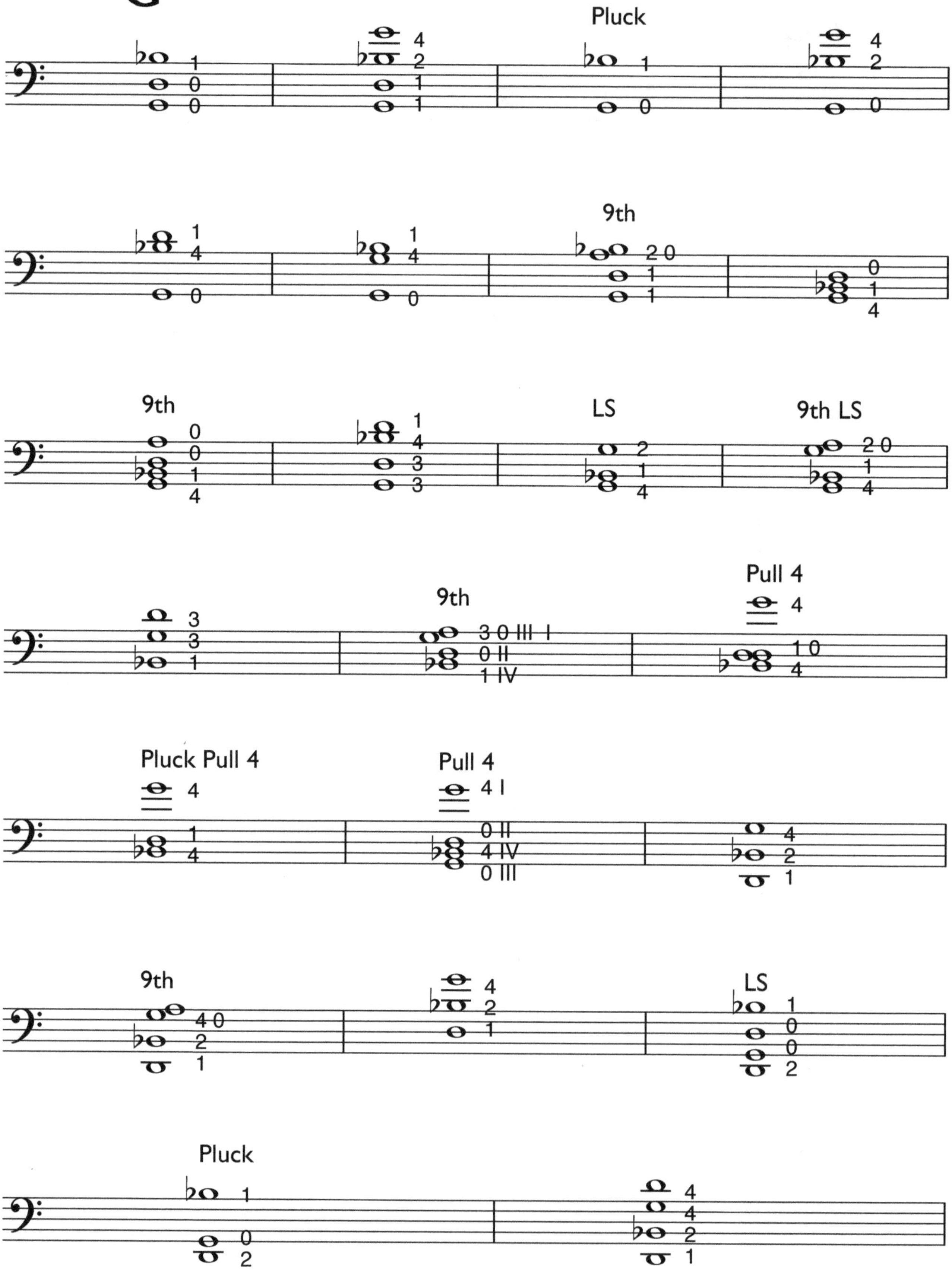
Pluck
9th
9th
LS
9th LS
9th
Pull 4
Pluck Pull 4
Pull 4
9th
LS
Pluck

G-7

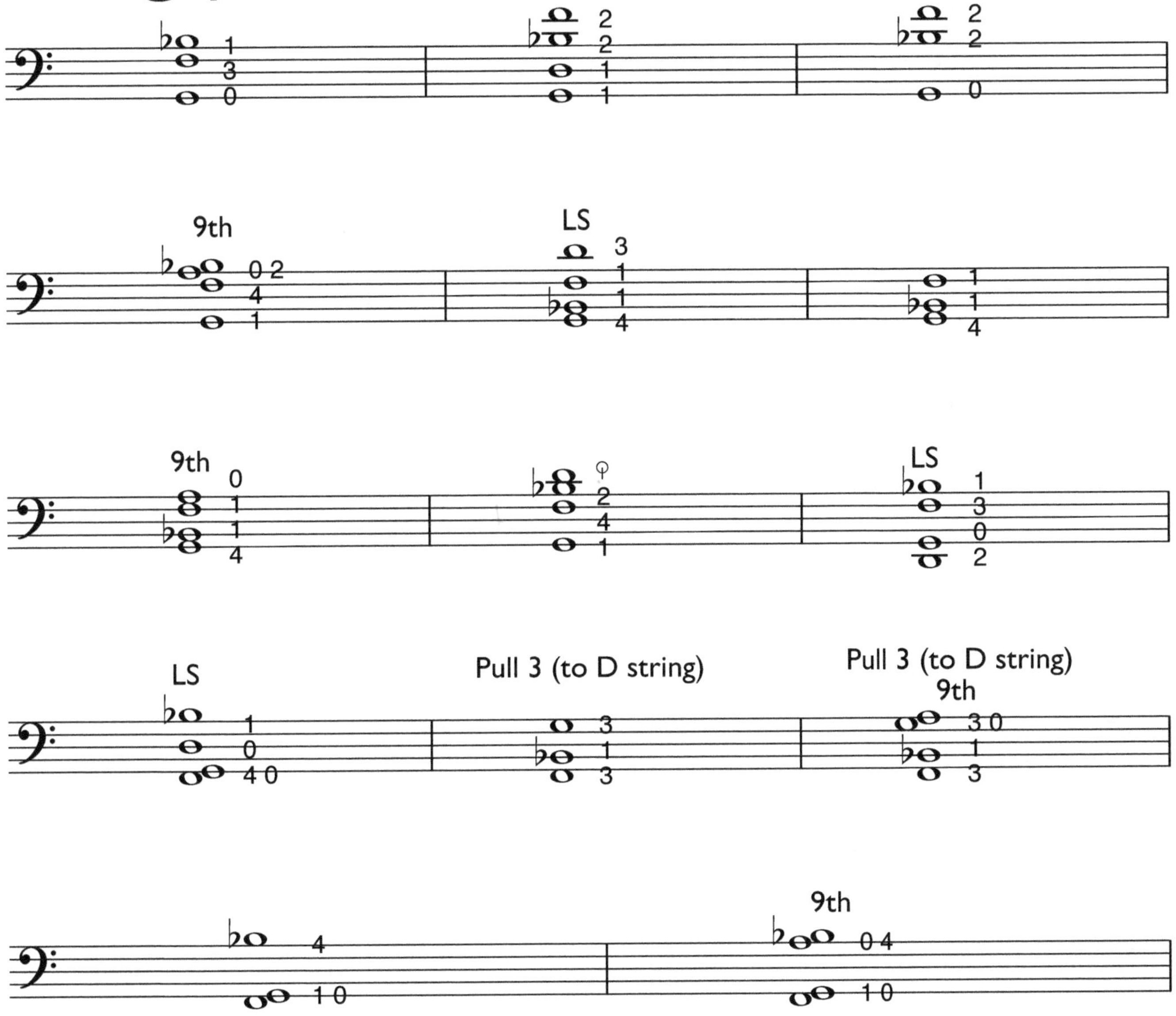
9th
LS
9th
LS
LS
Pull 3 (to D string)
Pull 3 (to D string)
9th
9th

G-Δ

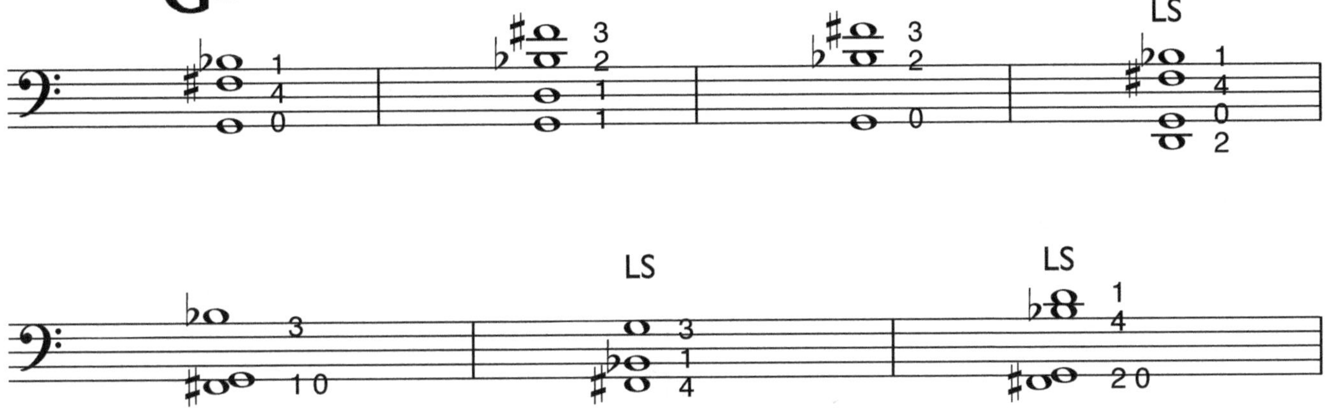
LS
LS
LS

23

D

D△7

D7

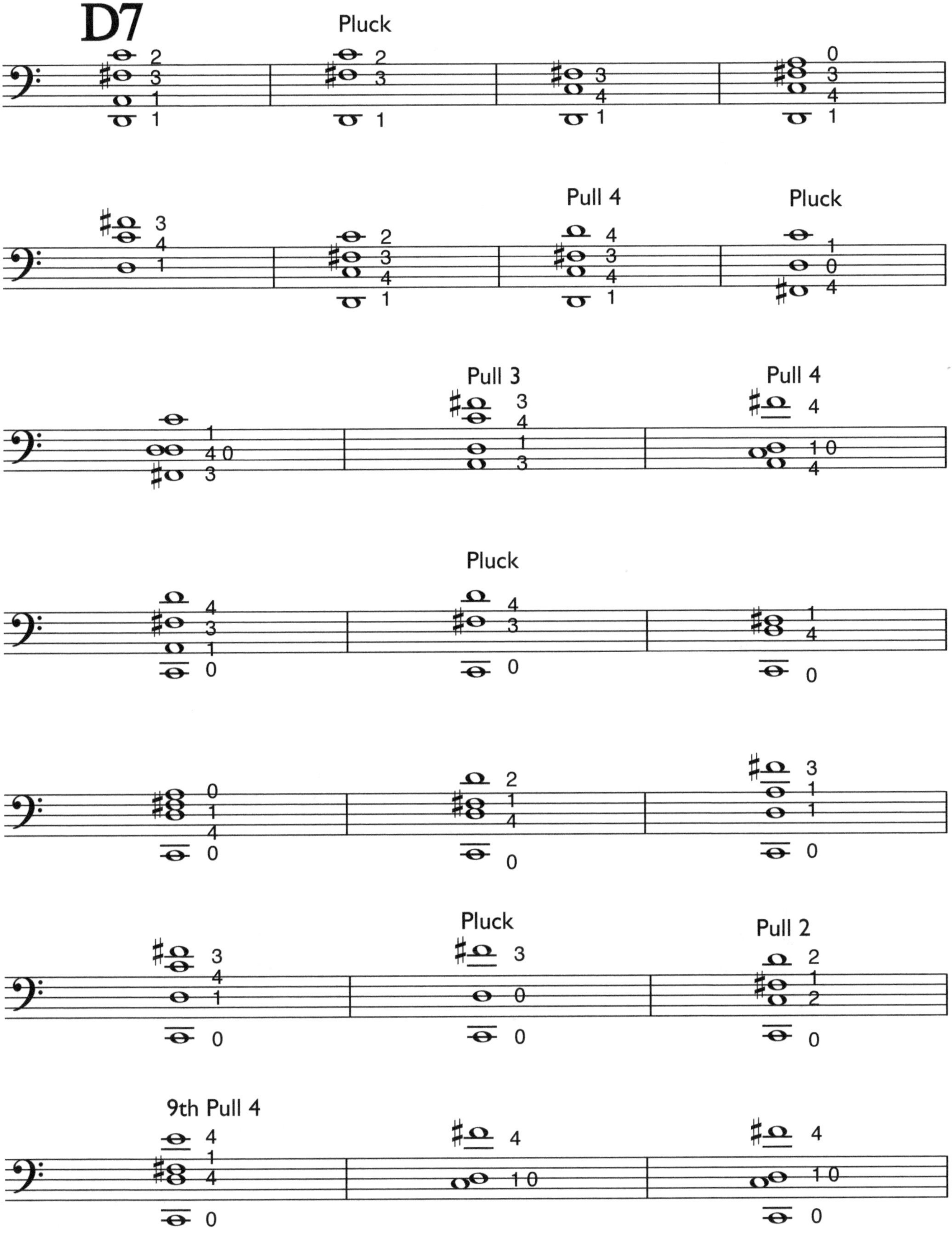

D+

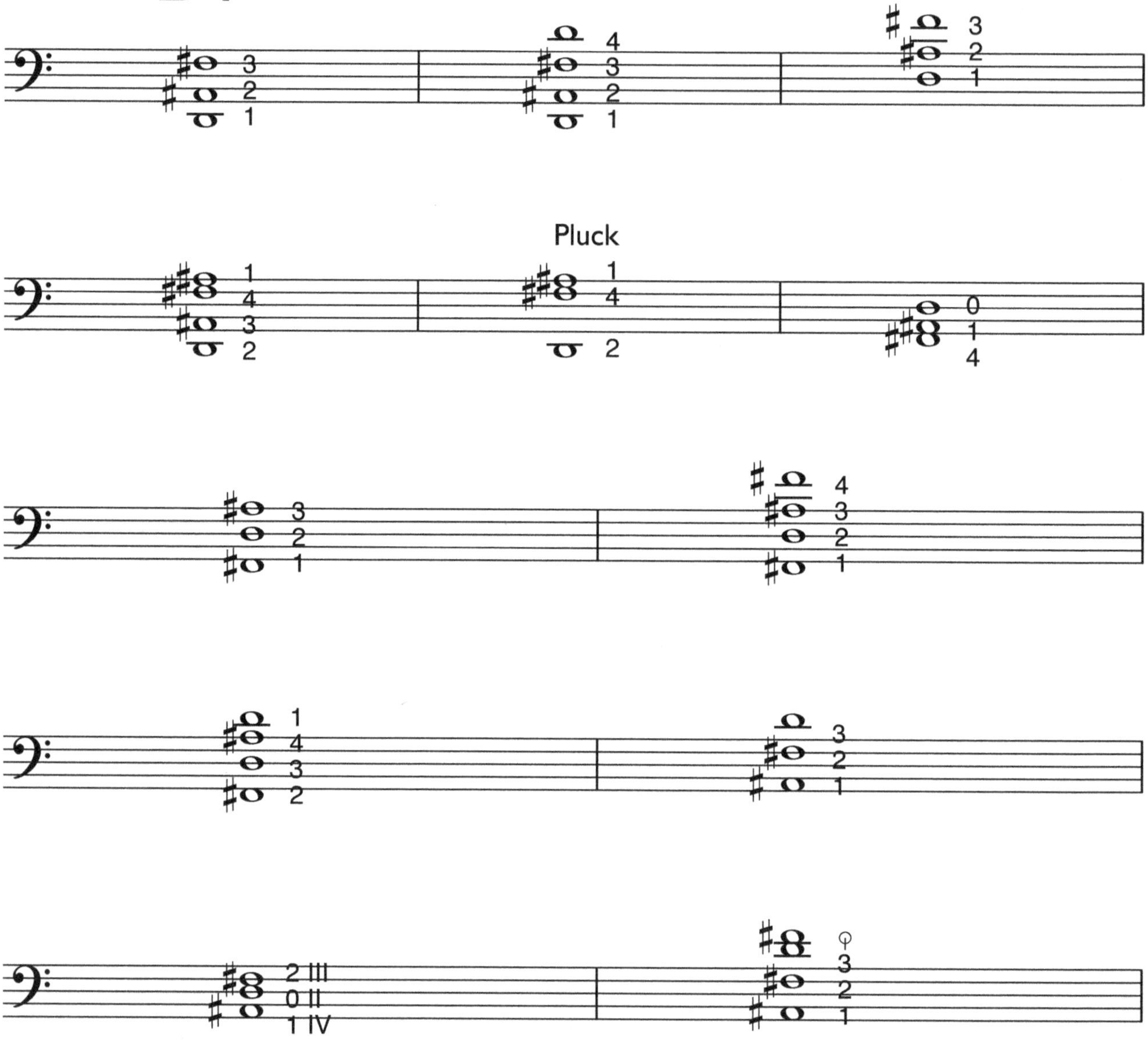

D+$^{\Delta}$

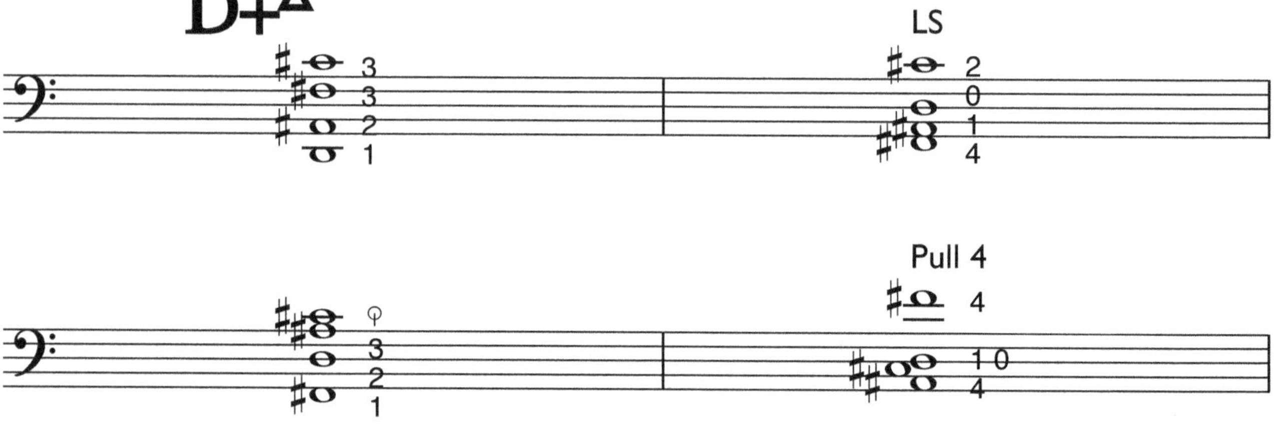

D-

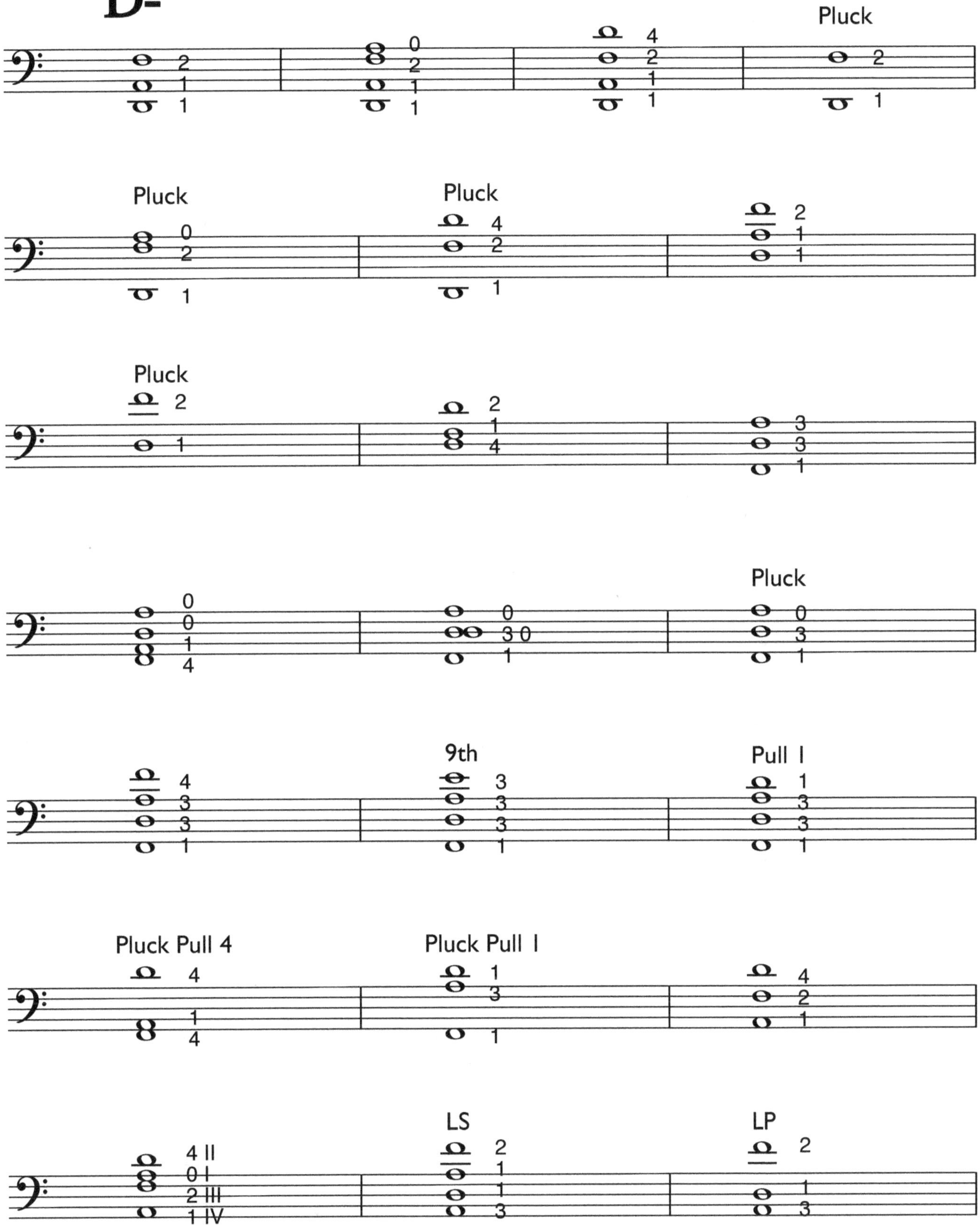
Pluck
Pluck
Pluck
Pluck
Pluck
9th
Pull 1
Pluck Pull 4
Pluck Pull 1
LS
LP

D-7

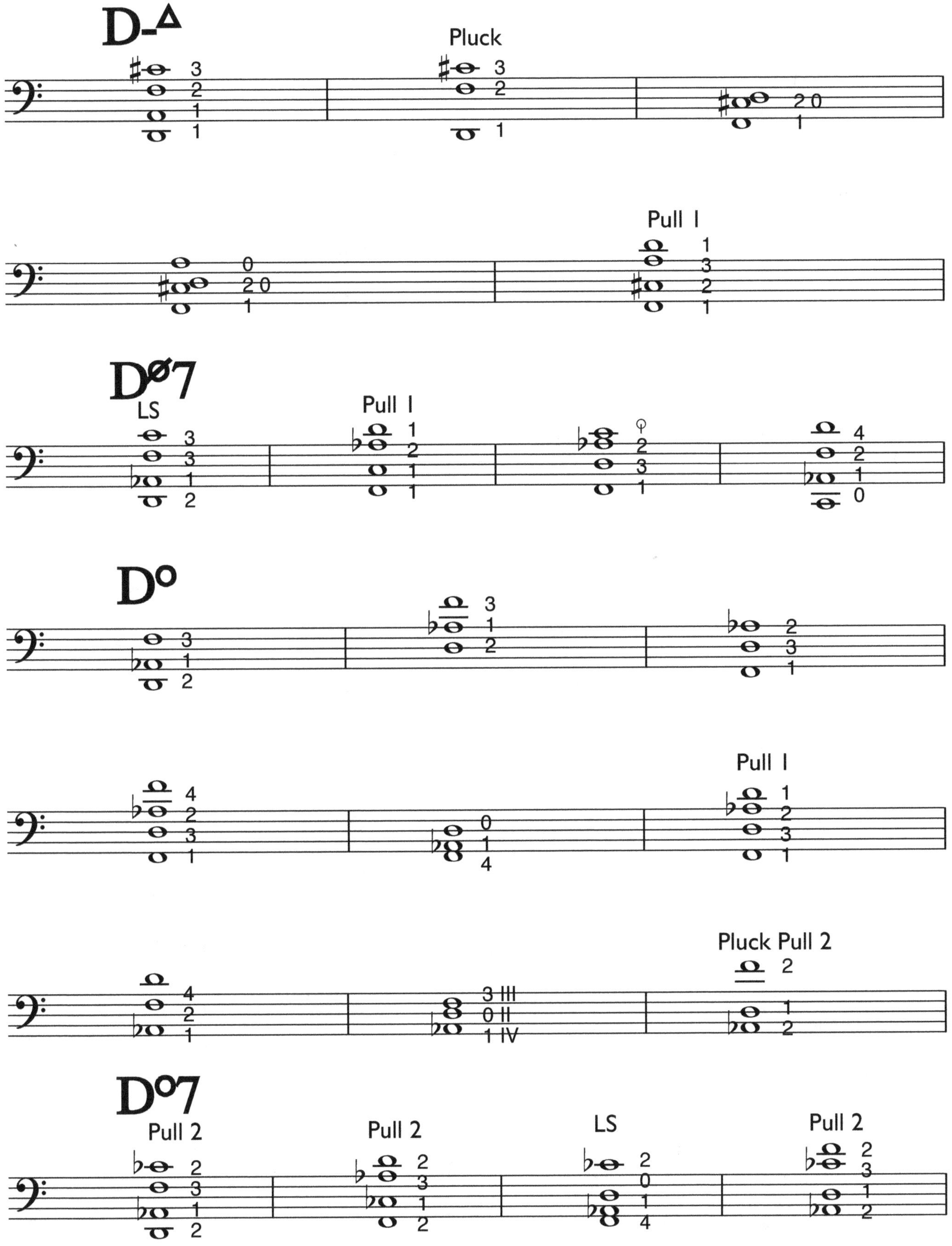
D-Δ
Pluck
Pull I
Dø7
LS
Pull I
D°
Pull I
Pluck Pull 2
D°7
Pull 2
Pull 2
LS
Pull 2

A

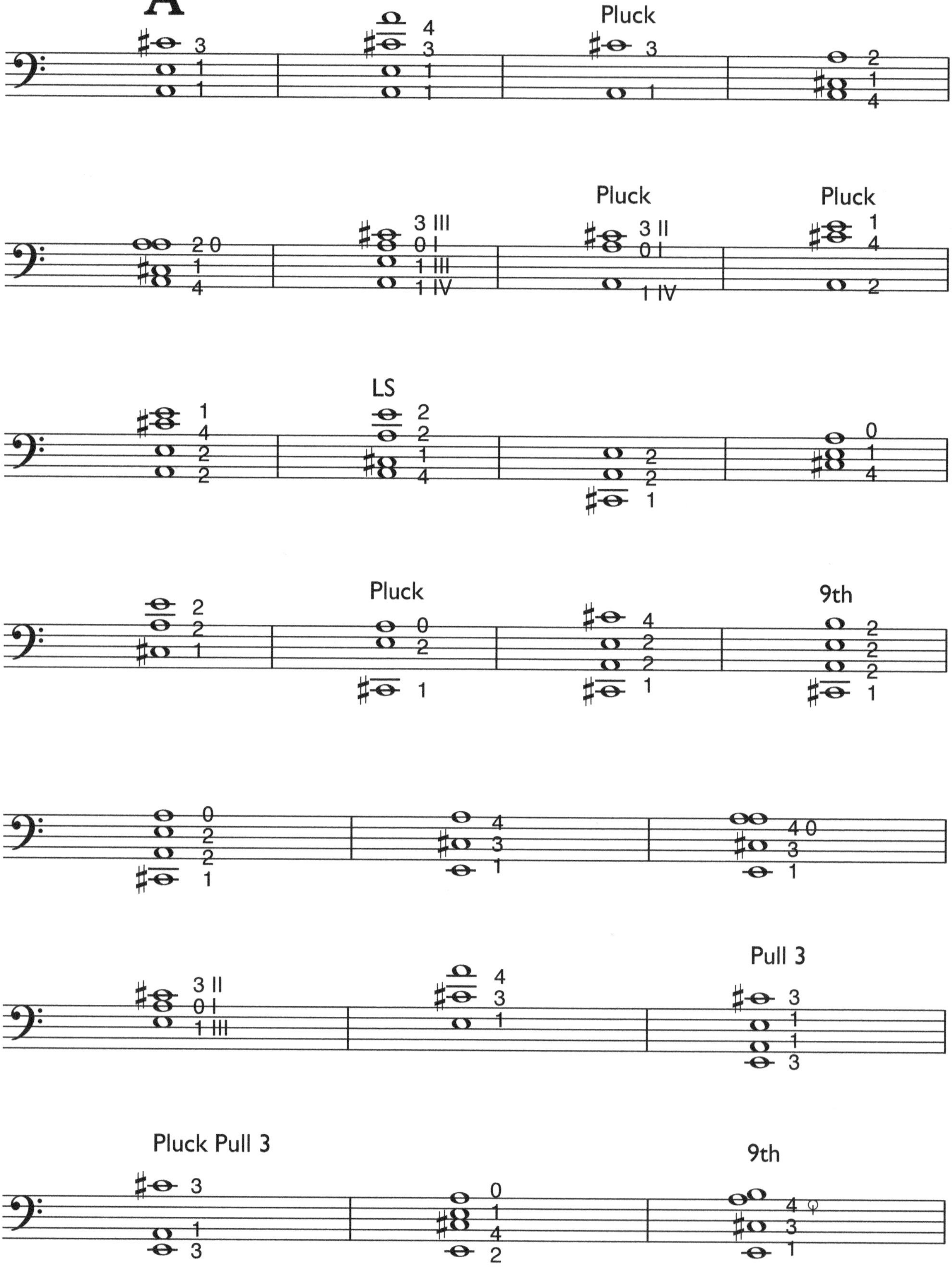

A△7

A7

32

A+

A+△
LS

A-

34

A-7

A-Δ

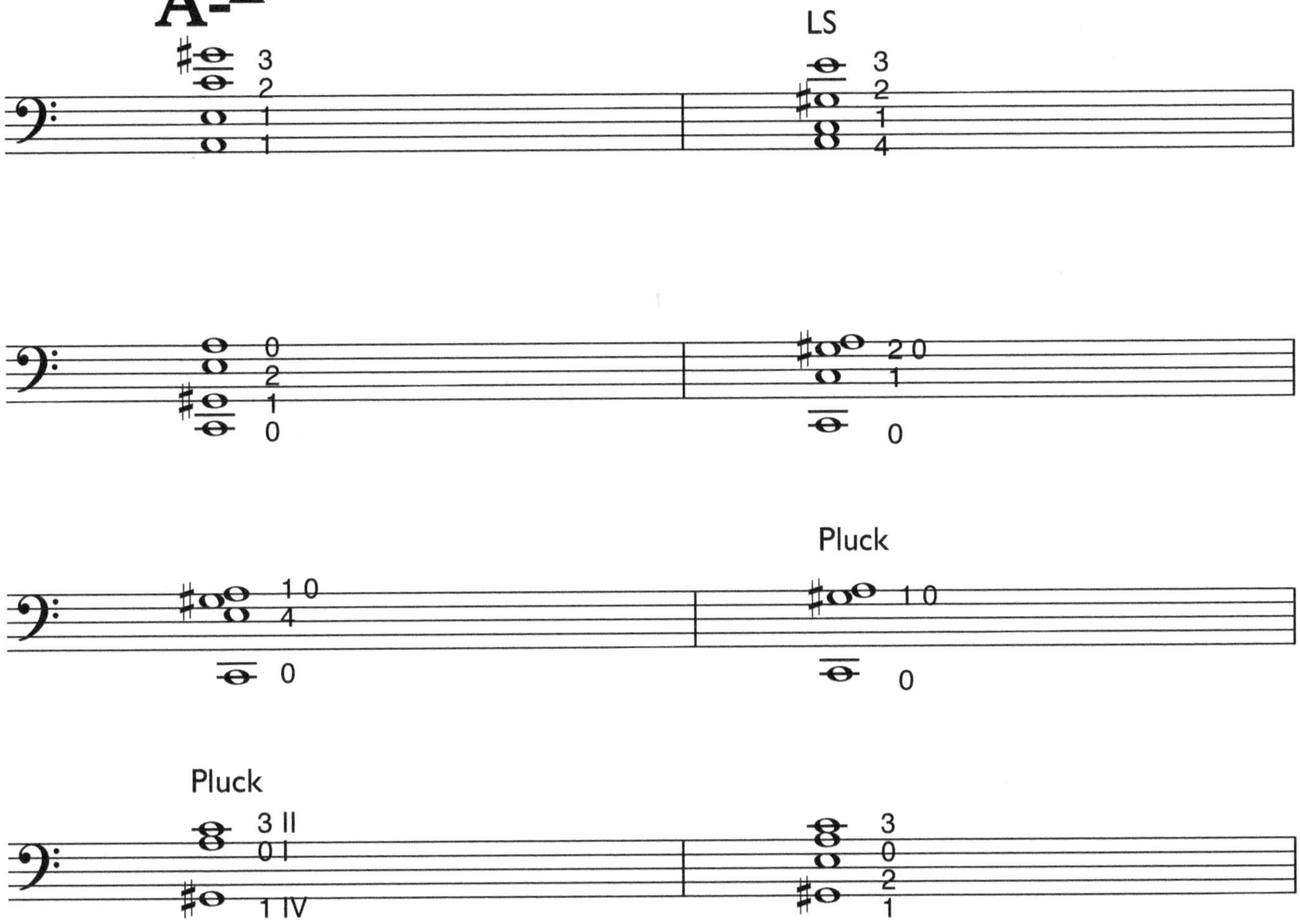

Aø7

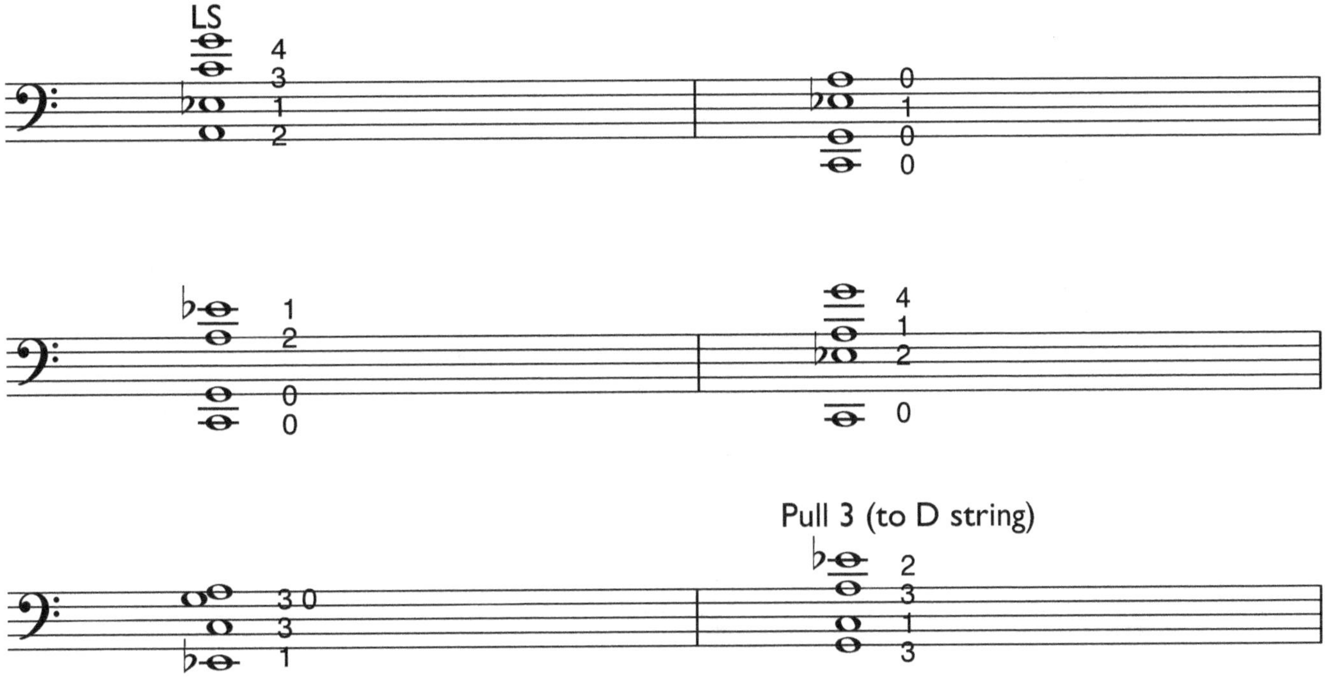

A°

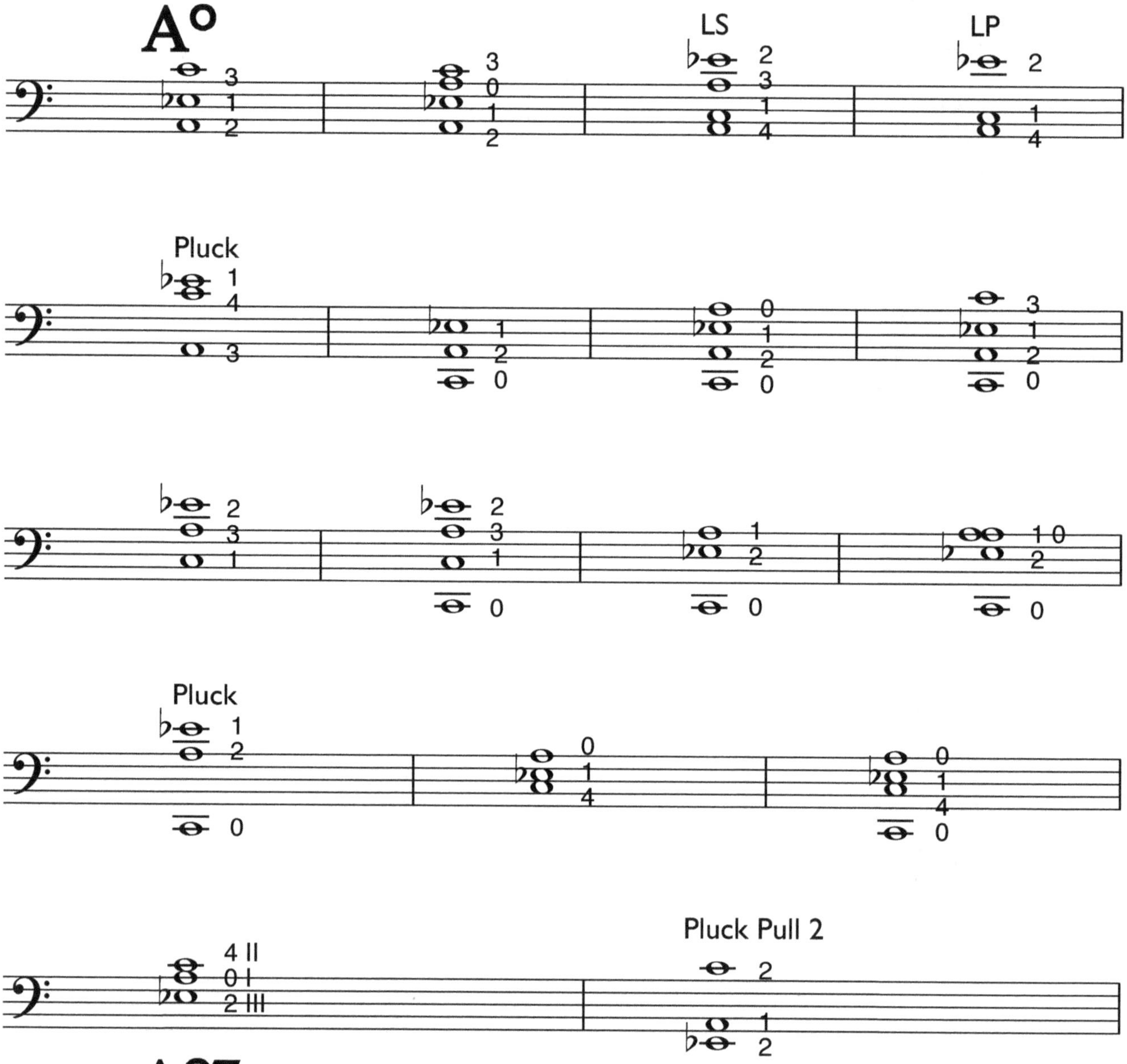

A°7

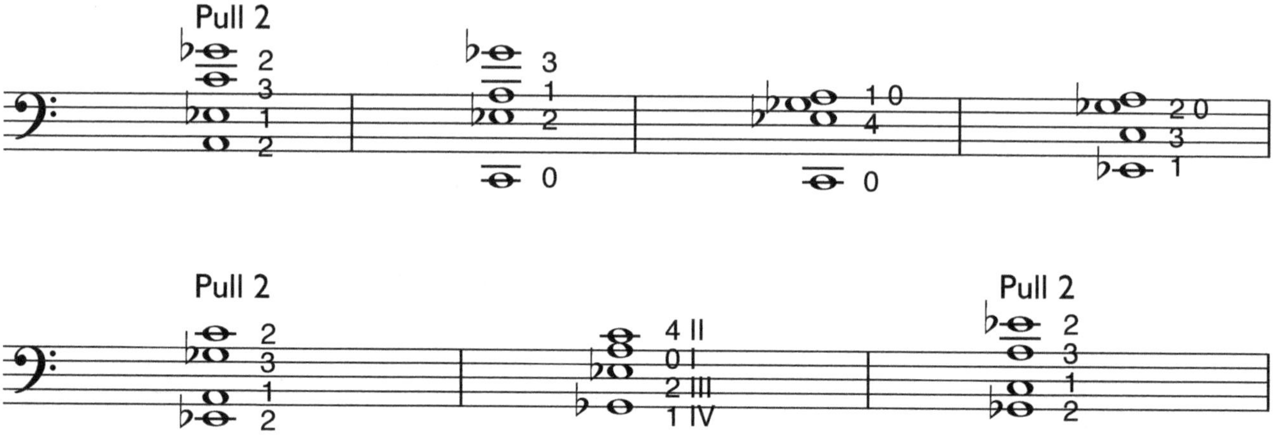

E

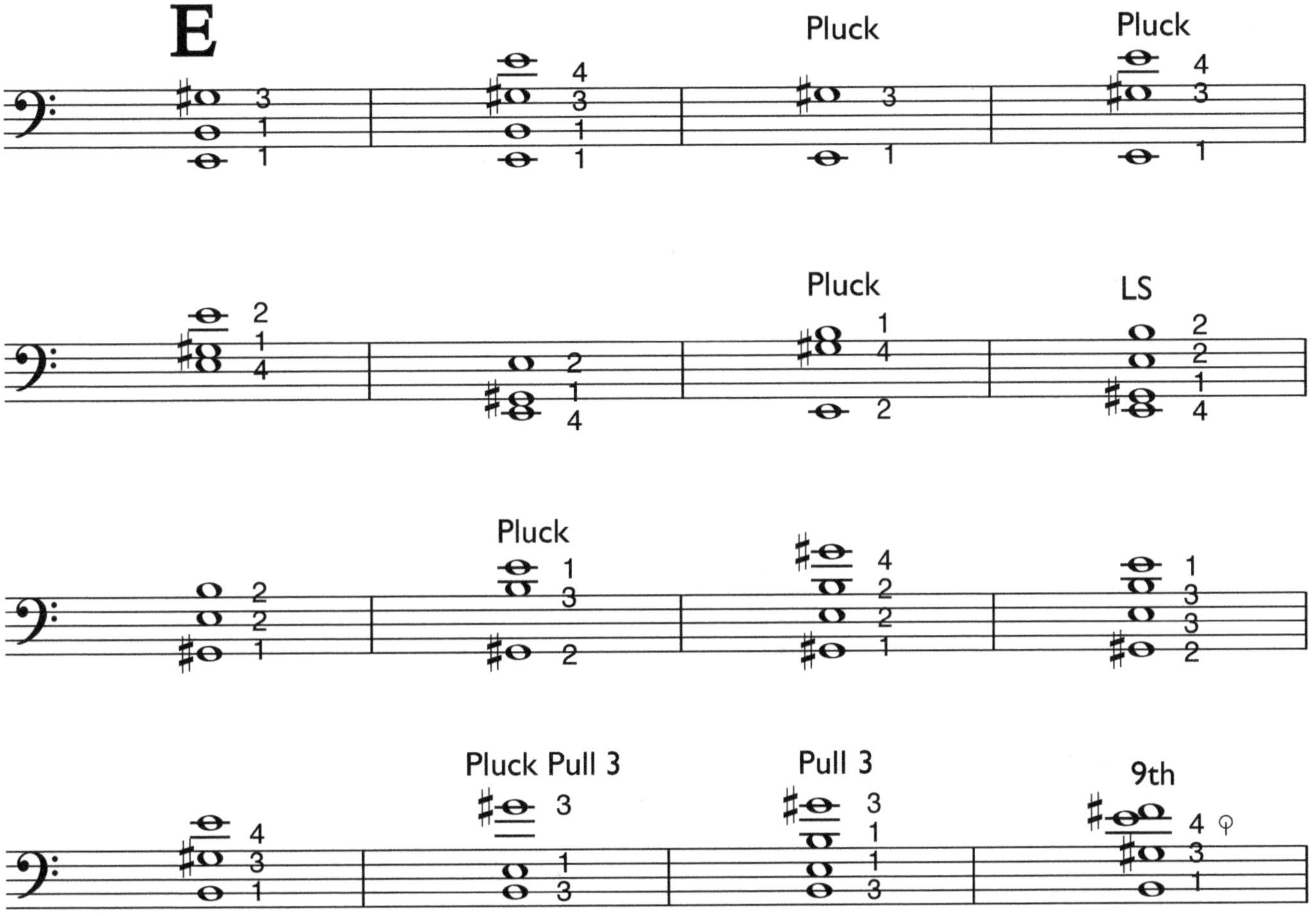

E$^{\Delta}$7

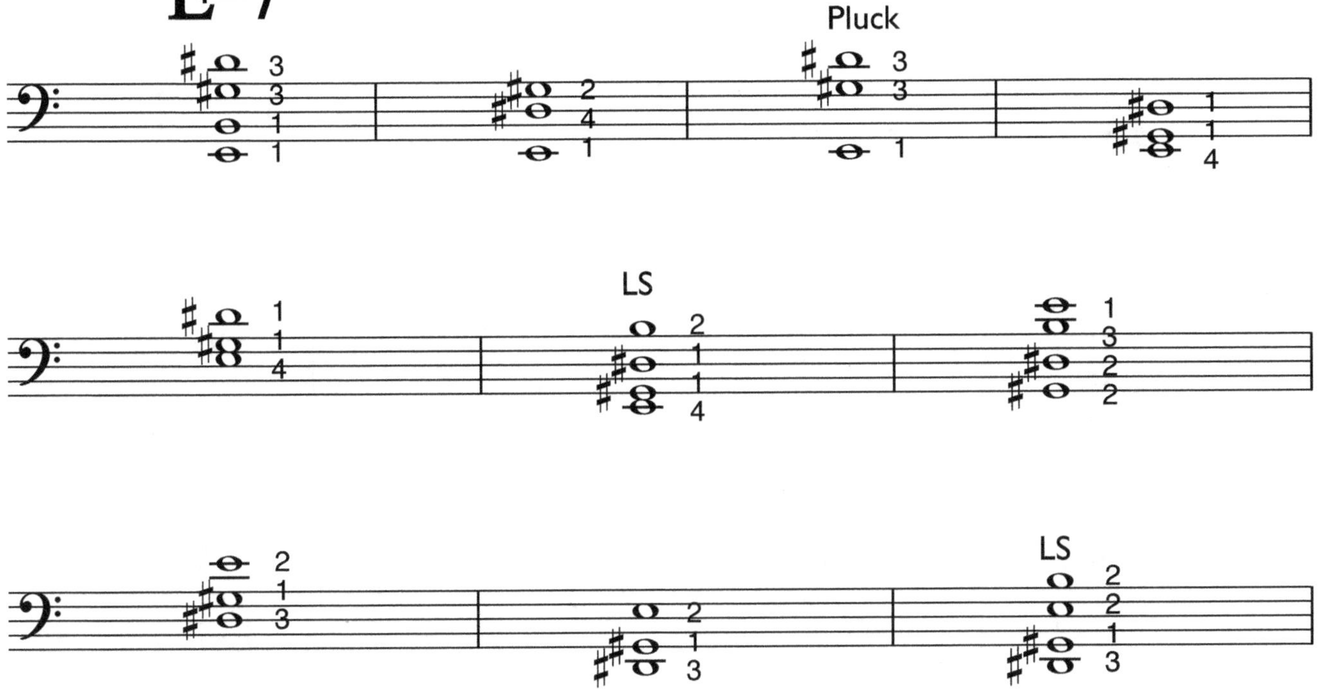

E7

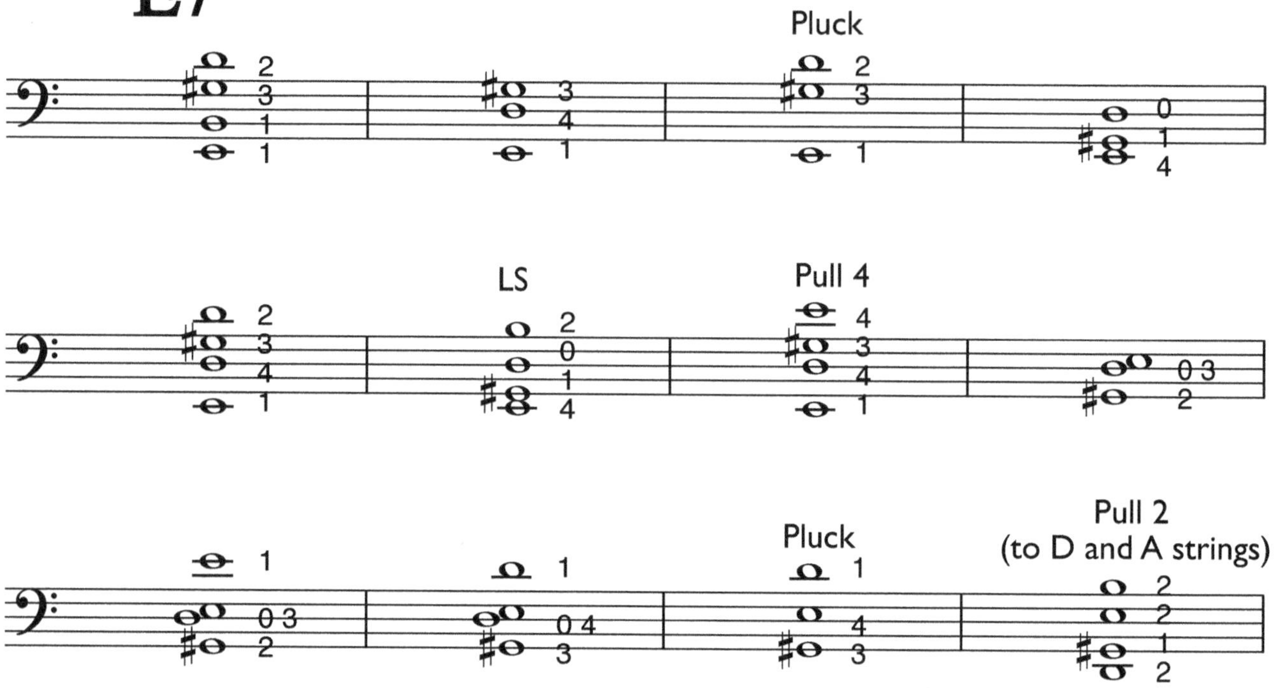
Pluck
LS
Pull 4
Pluck
Pull 2
(to D and A strings)

E+

Pluck
Pluck
Pluck
Pluck

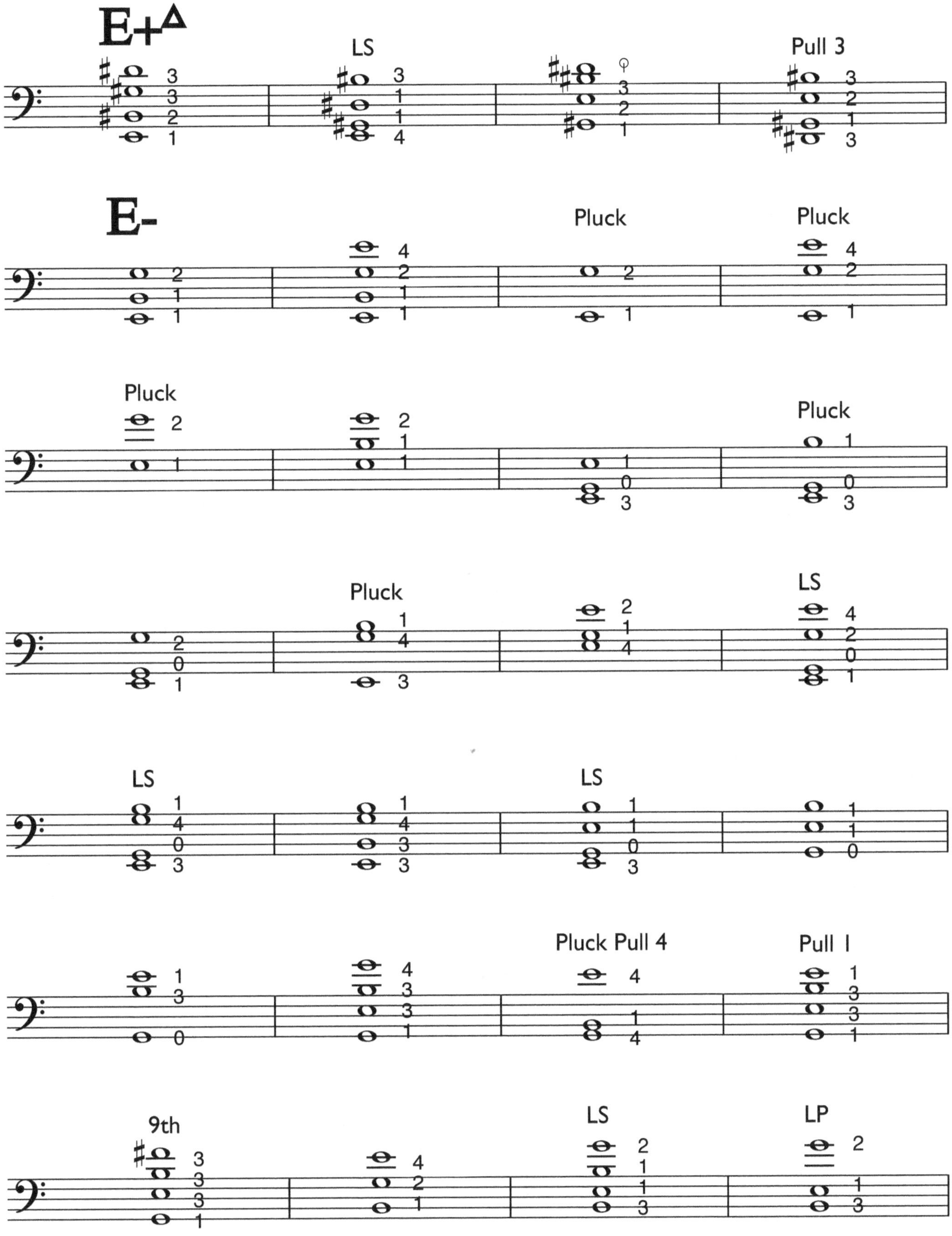
E+Δ
LS
Pull 3
E-
Pluck
Pluck
Pluck
Pluck
Pluck
LS
LS
LS
Pluck Pull 4
Pull 1
9th
LS
LP

E-7

Pull 4

Pull 1 (to D string)

Pull 1 (to D string)

Pull 1
(to D and A strings)

E-△

Pluck

LS

LS

LS

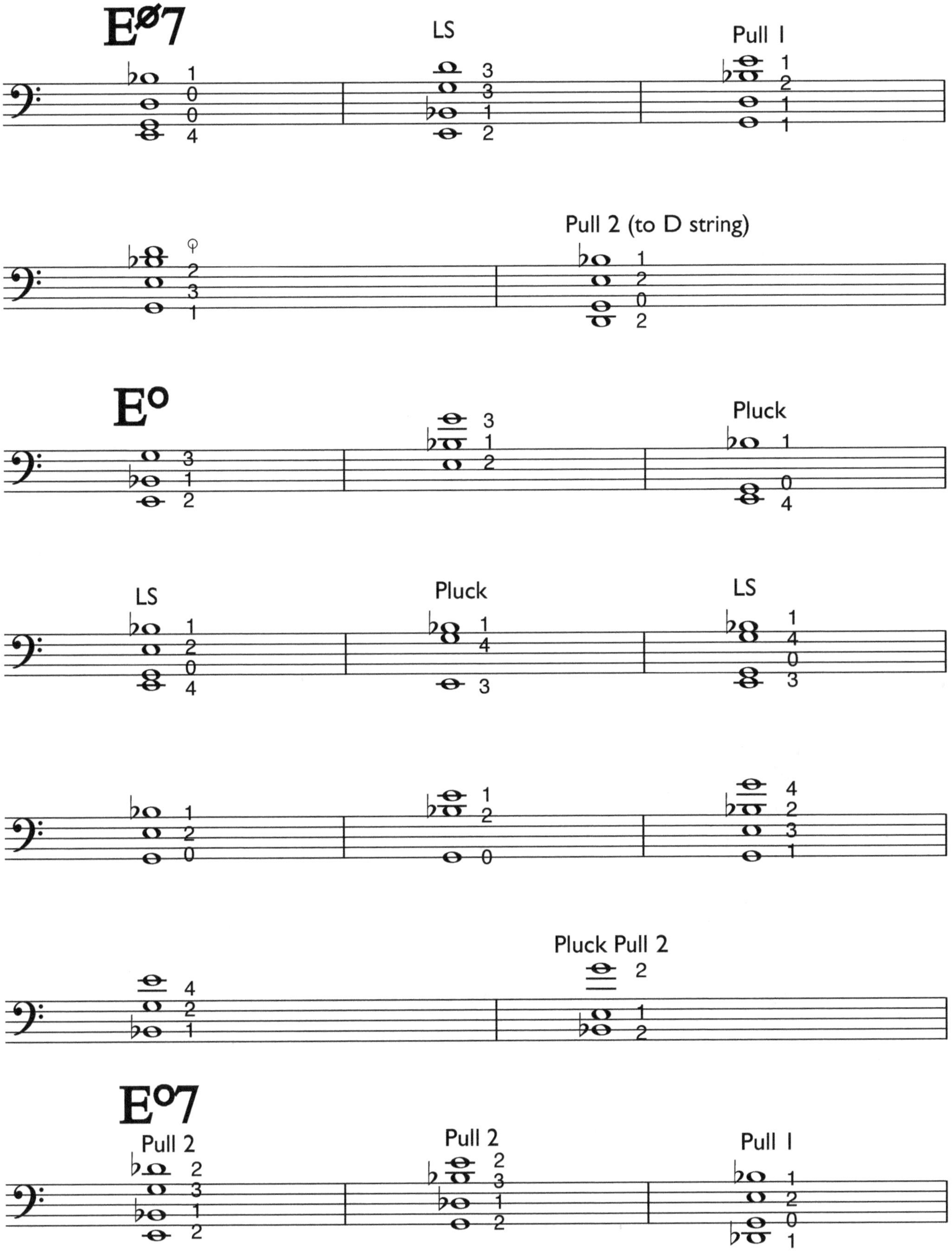
Eø7
LS
Pull 1
Pull 2 (to D string)
E°
Pluck
LS
Pluck
LS
Pluck Pull 2
E°7
Pull 2
Pull 2
Pull 1

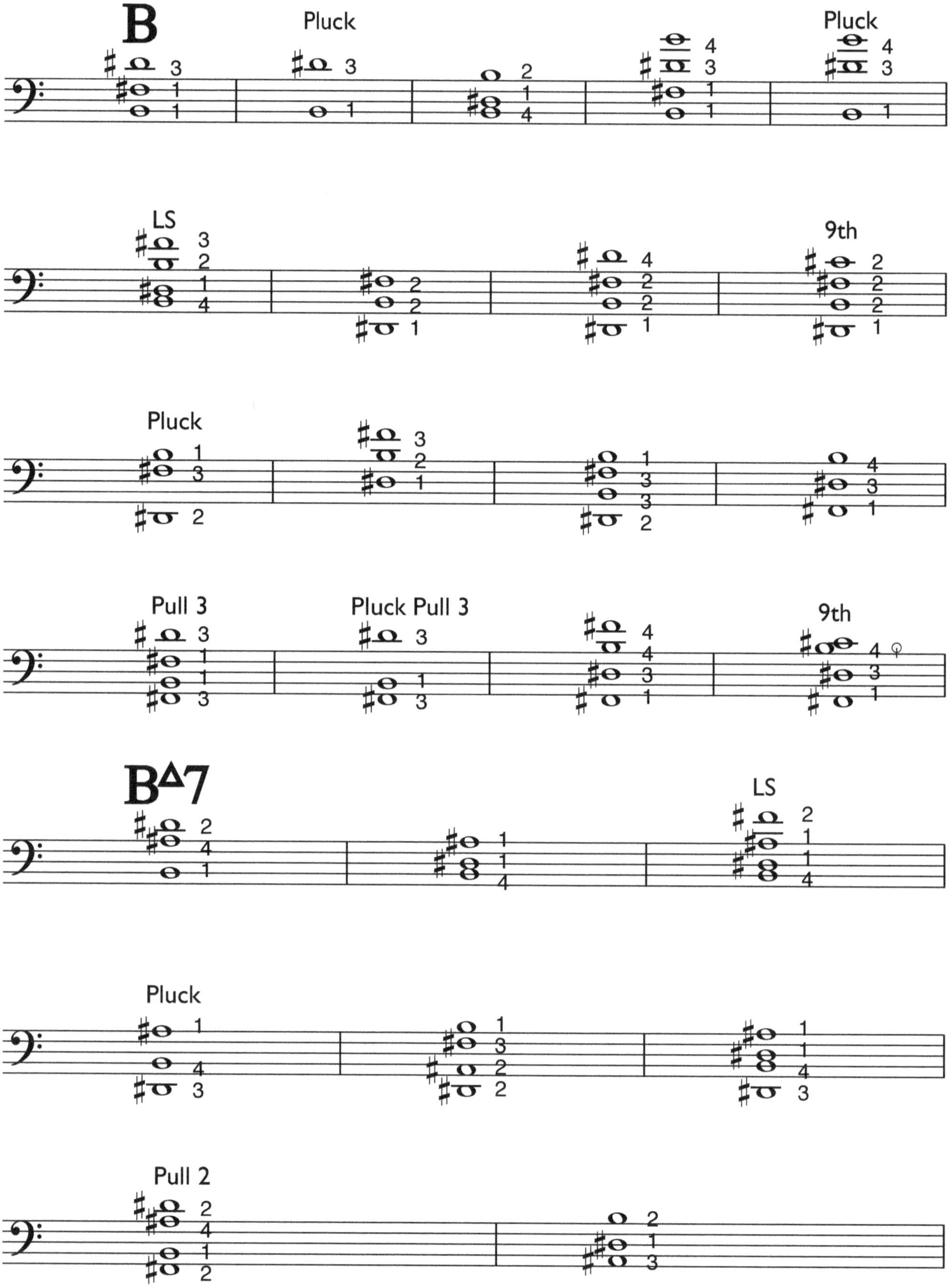
B
Pluck
Pluck
LS
9th
Pluck
Pull 3
Pluck Pull 3
9th
B△7
LS
Pluck
Pull 2

B7

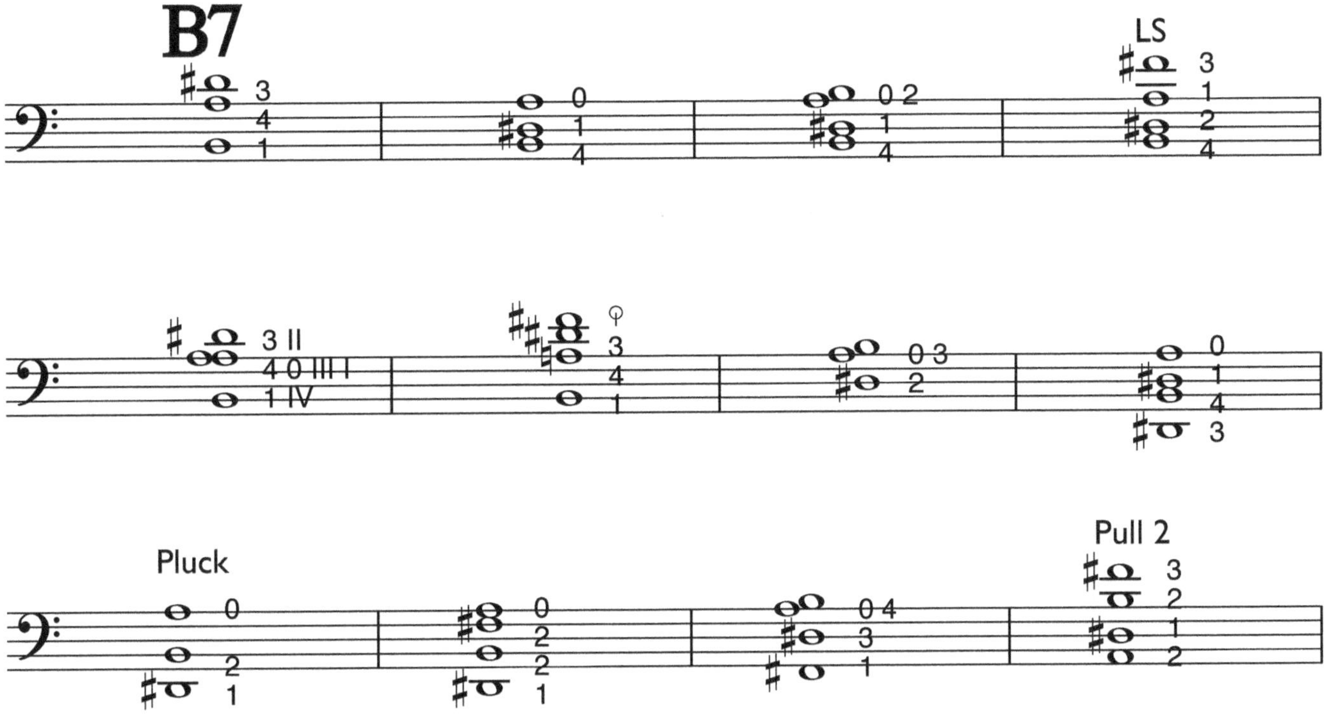

B+

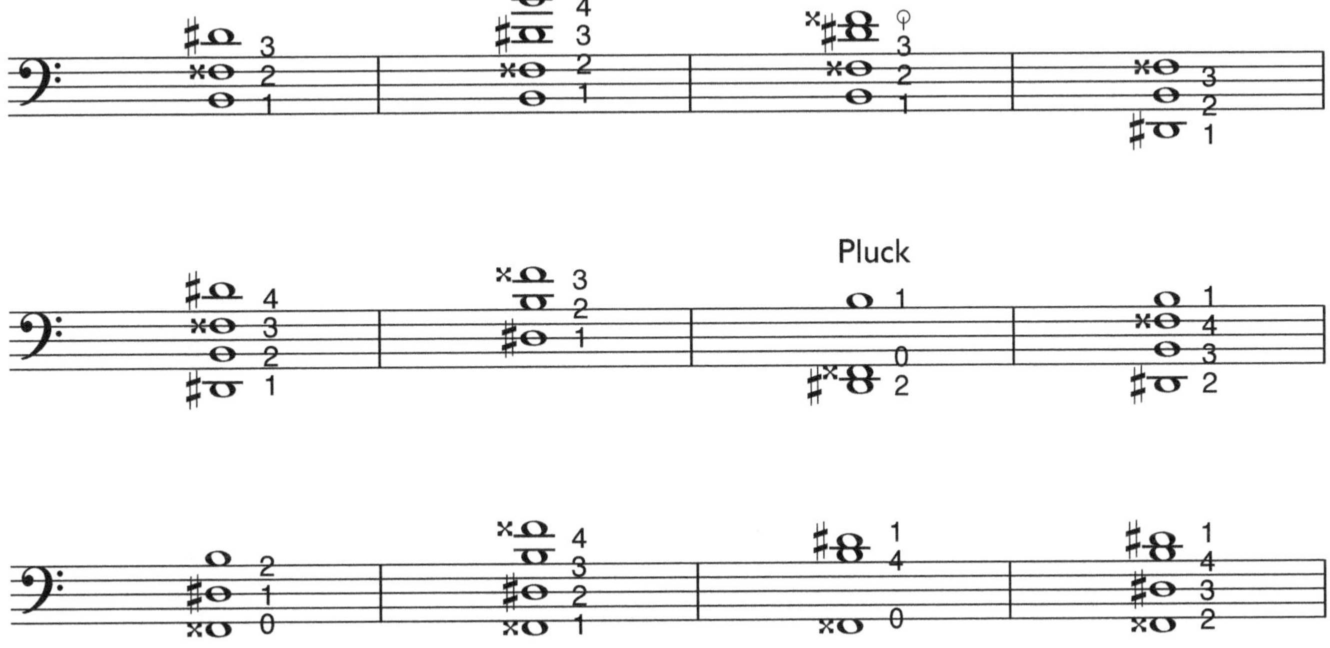

B+Δ

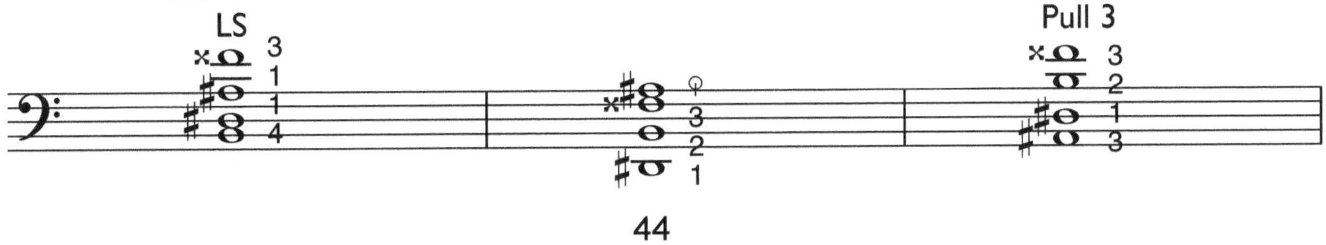

B-

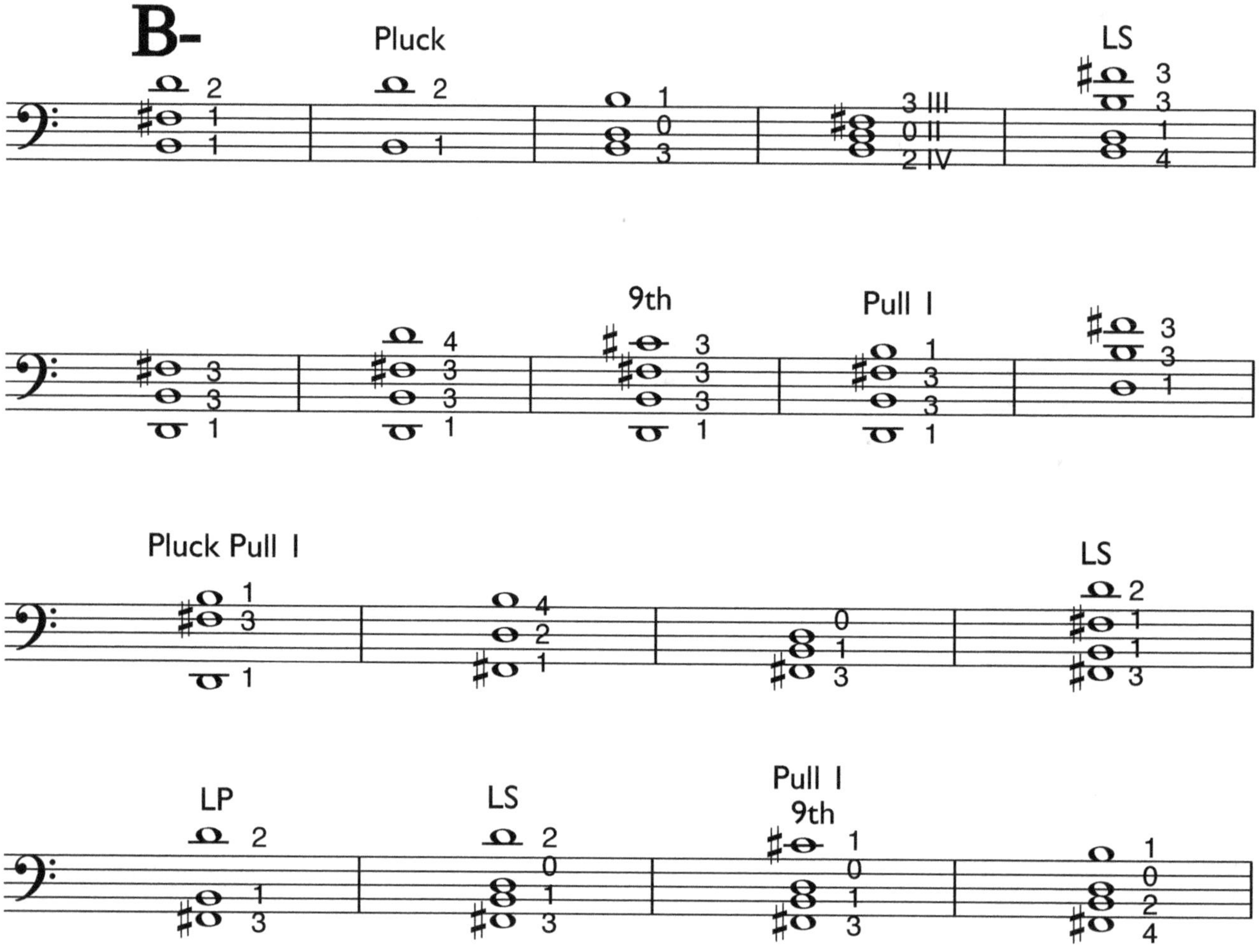
Pluck
LS
9th
Pull I
Pluck Pull I
LS
LP
LS
Pull I
9th

B-7

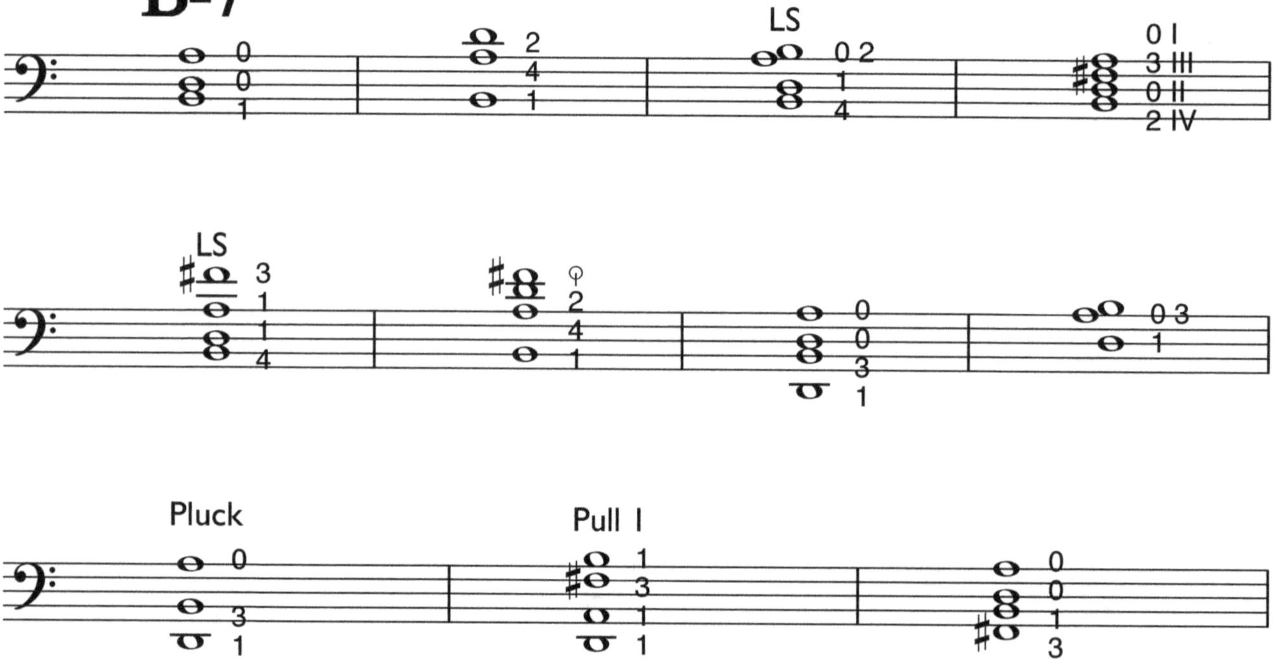
LS
LS
Pluck
Pull I

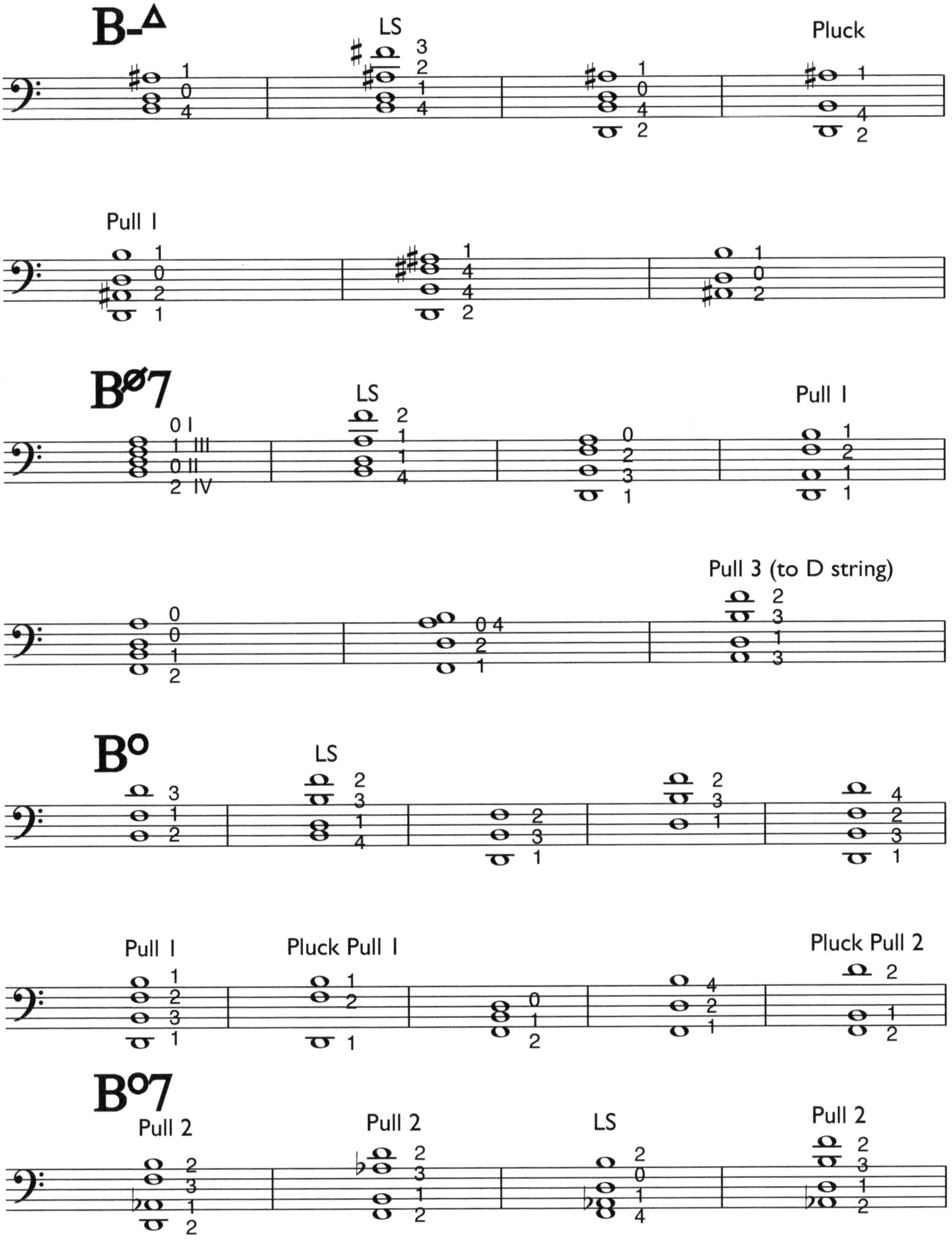
B-Δ
LS
Pluck
Pull 1
Bø7
LS
Pull 1
Pull 3 (to D string)
B°
LS
Pull 1
Pluck Pull 1
Pluck Pull 2
B°7
Pull 2
Pull 2
LS
Pull 2

F♯

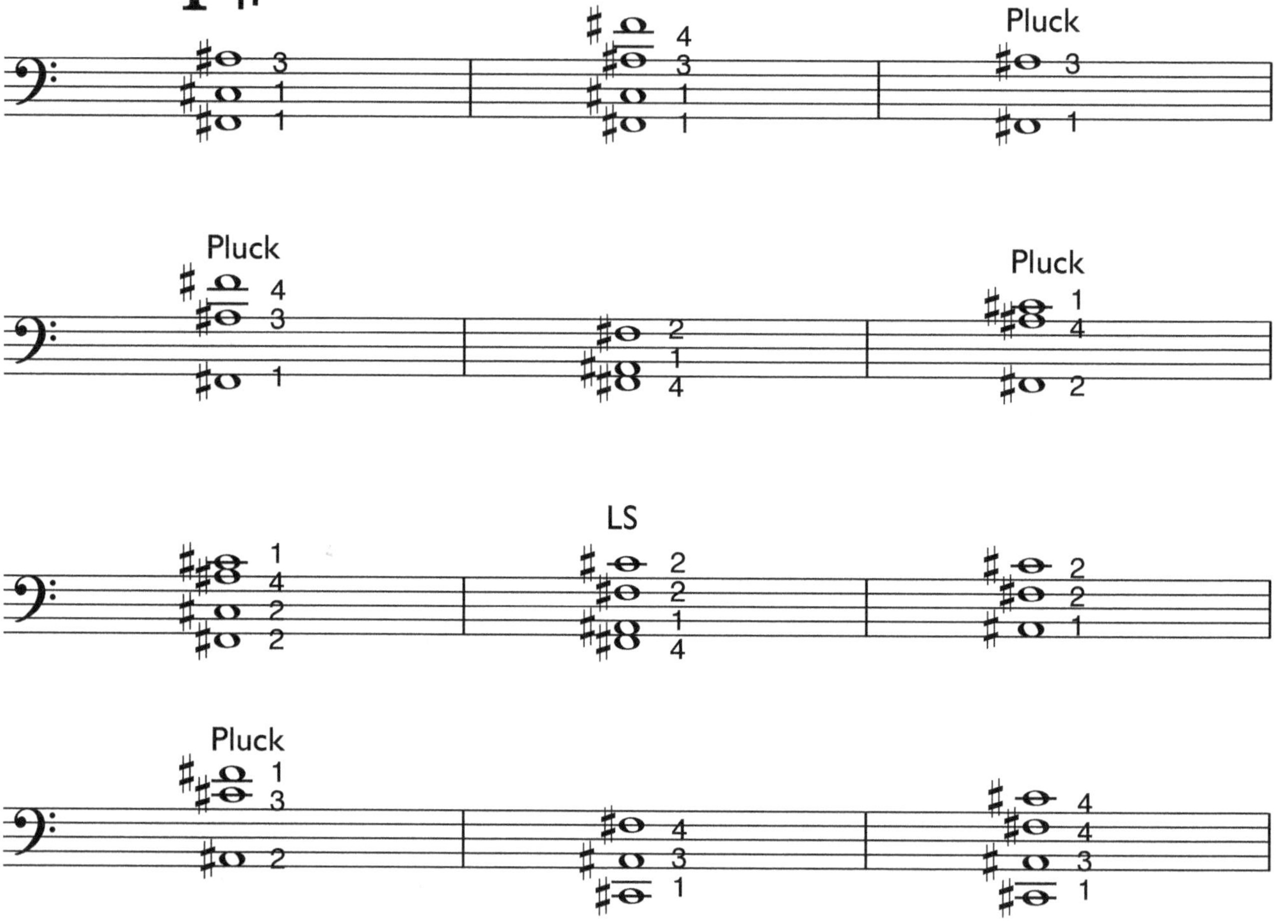

F♯Δ7

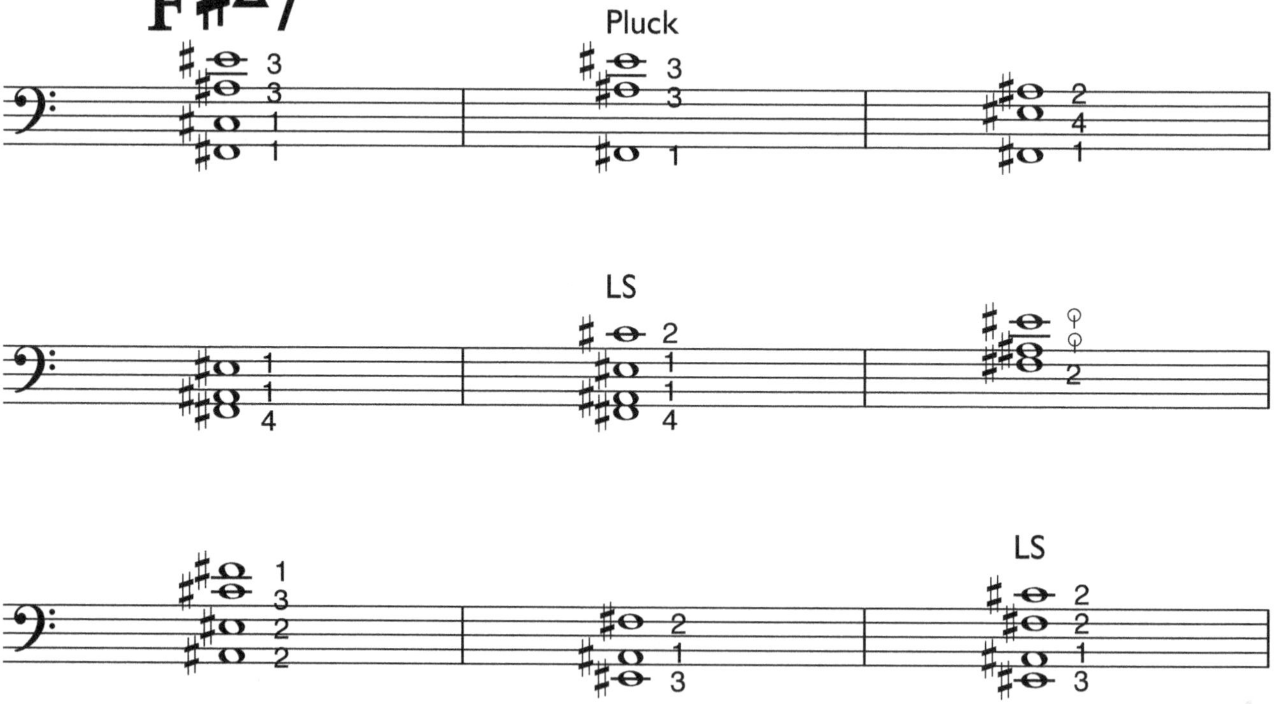

48

F#+△

F#-

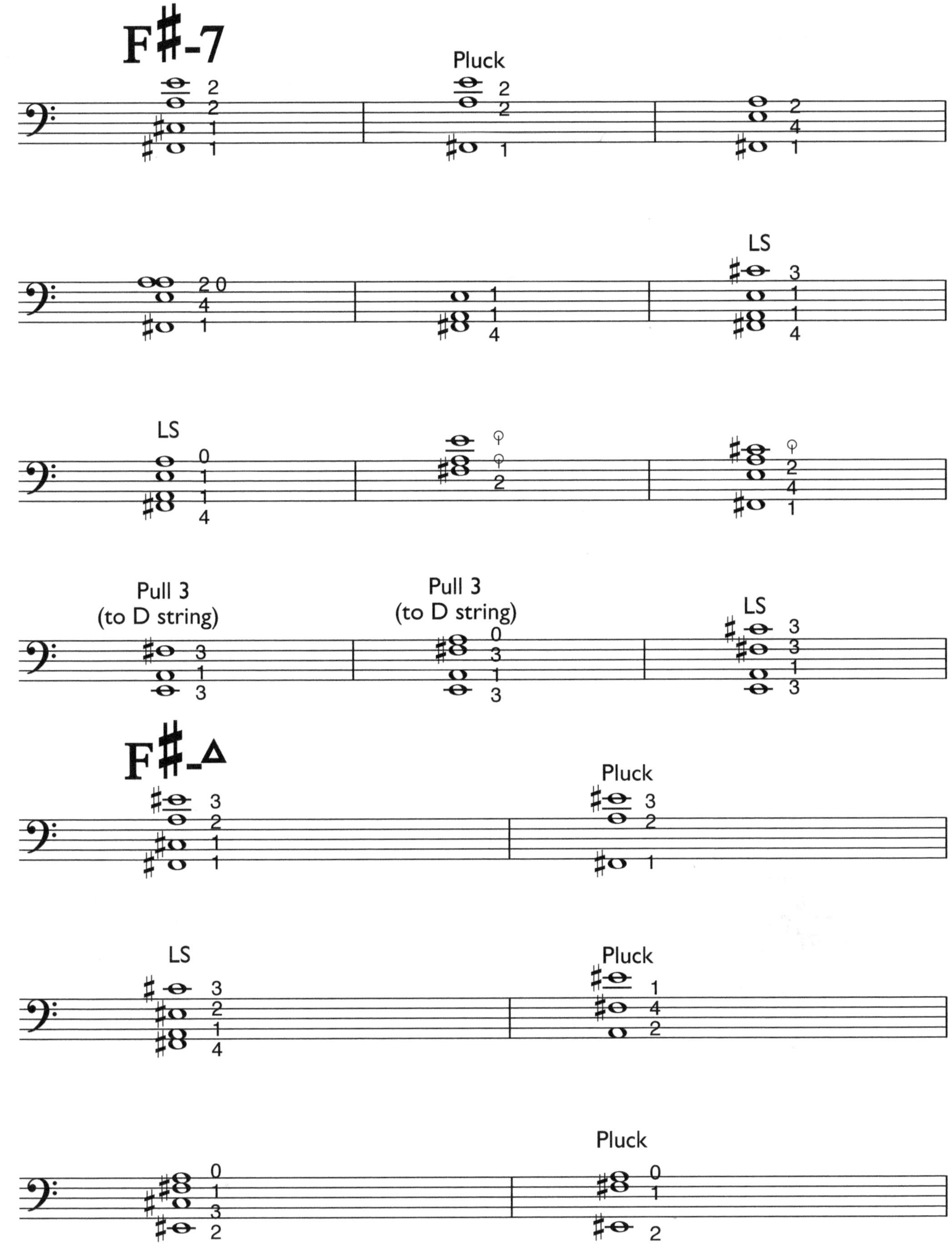
F♯-7
Pluck
LS
LS
Pull 3
(to D string)
Pull 3
(to D string)
LS
F♯-Δ
Pluck
LS
Pluck
Pluck

51

D♭

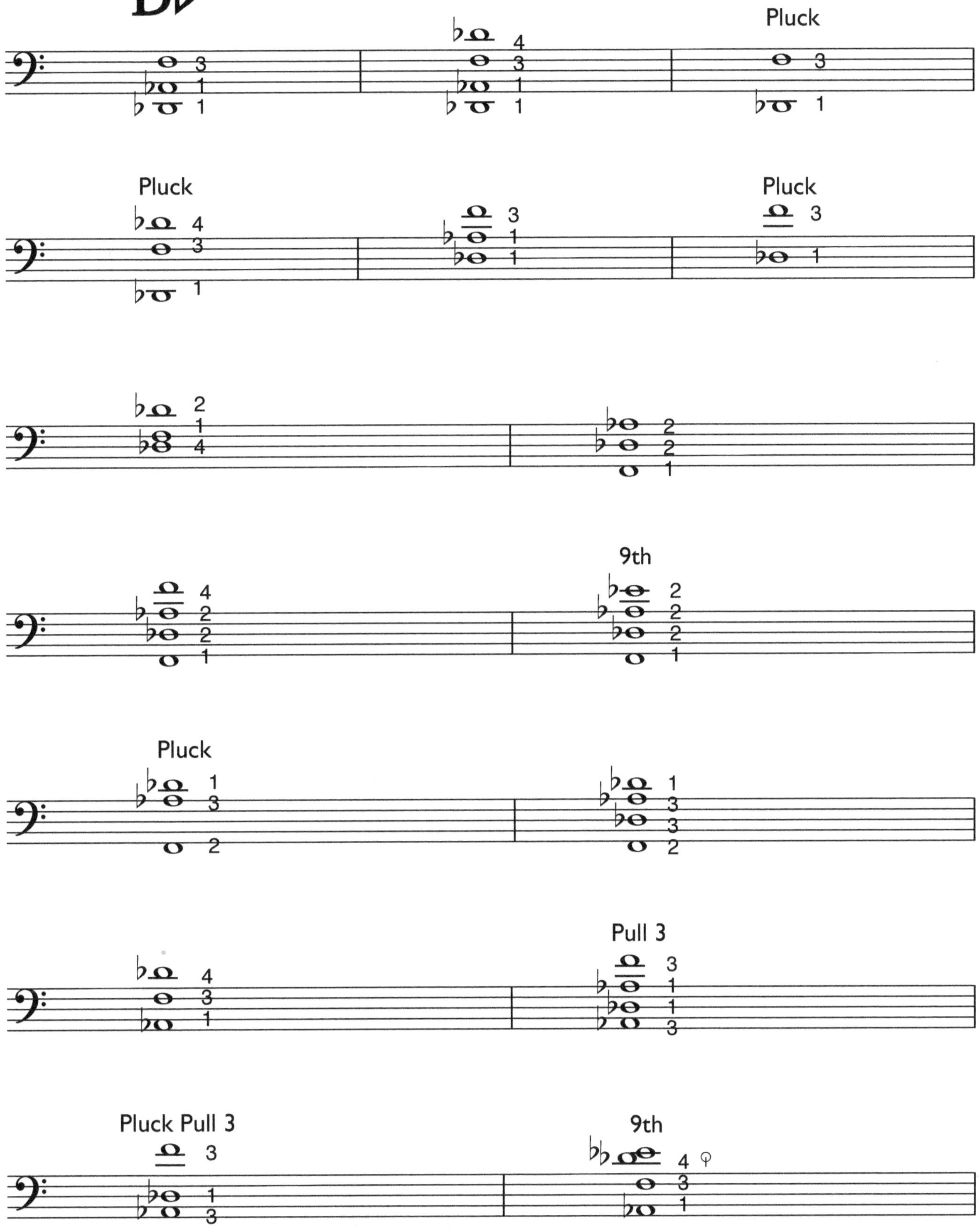

D♭△7

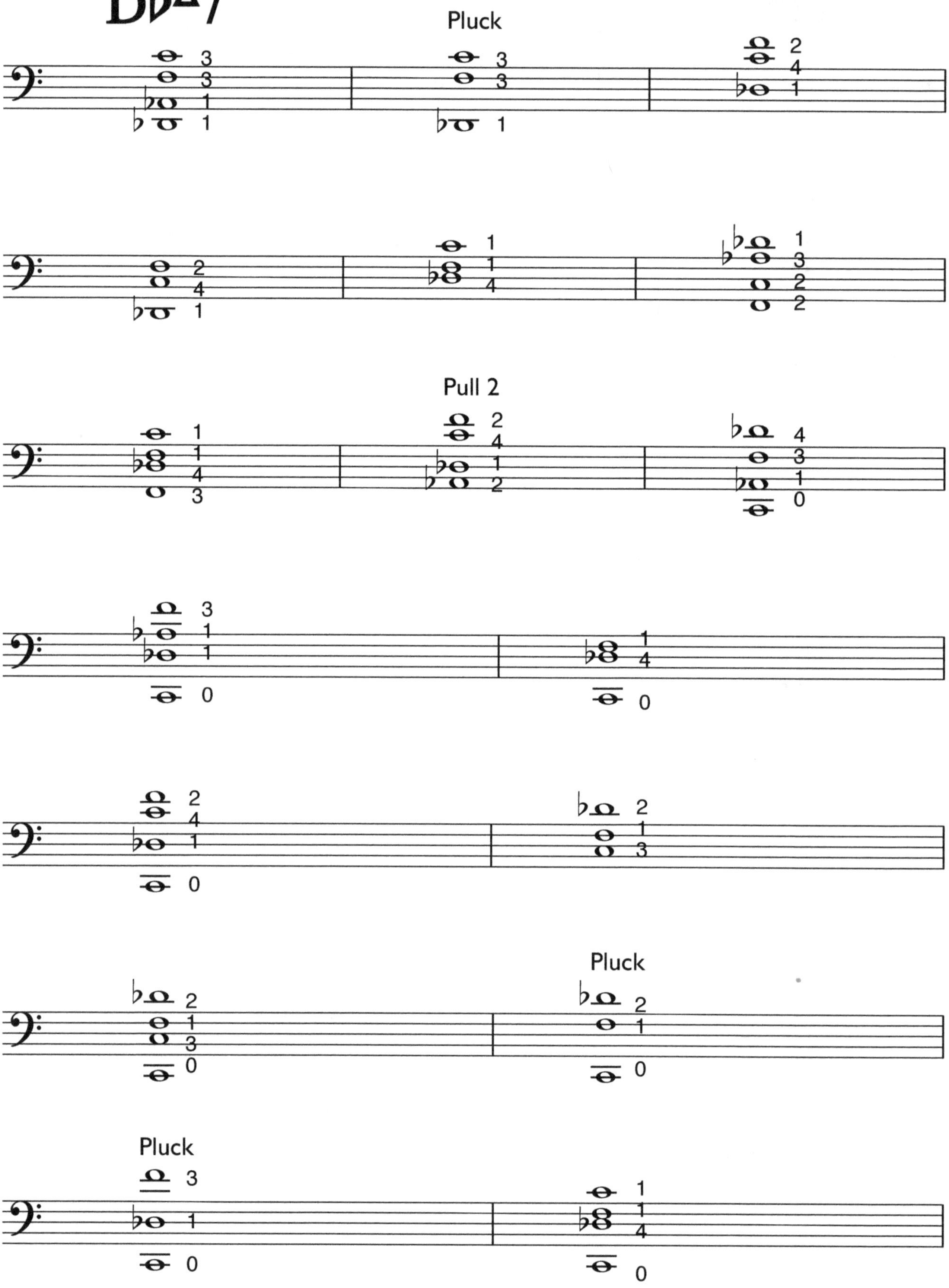

D♭7

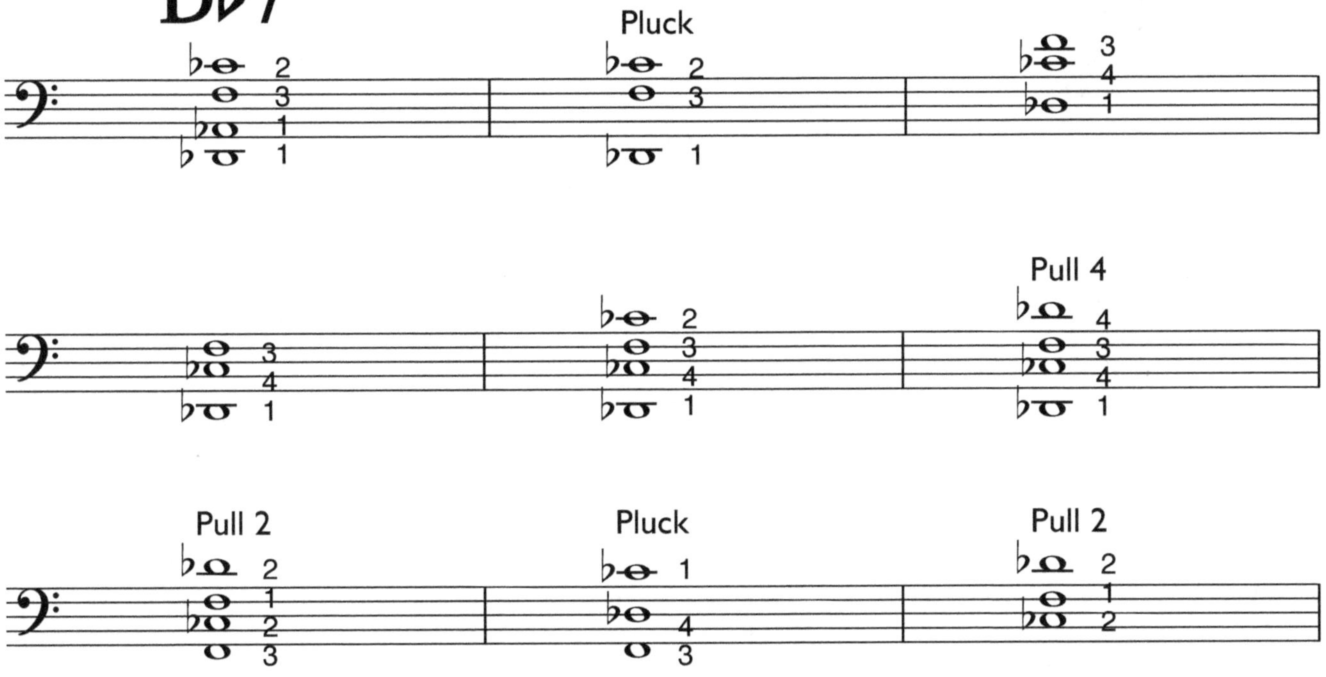

D♭+

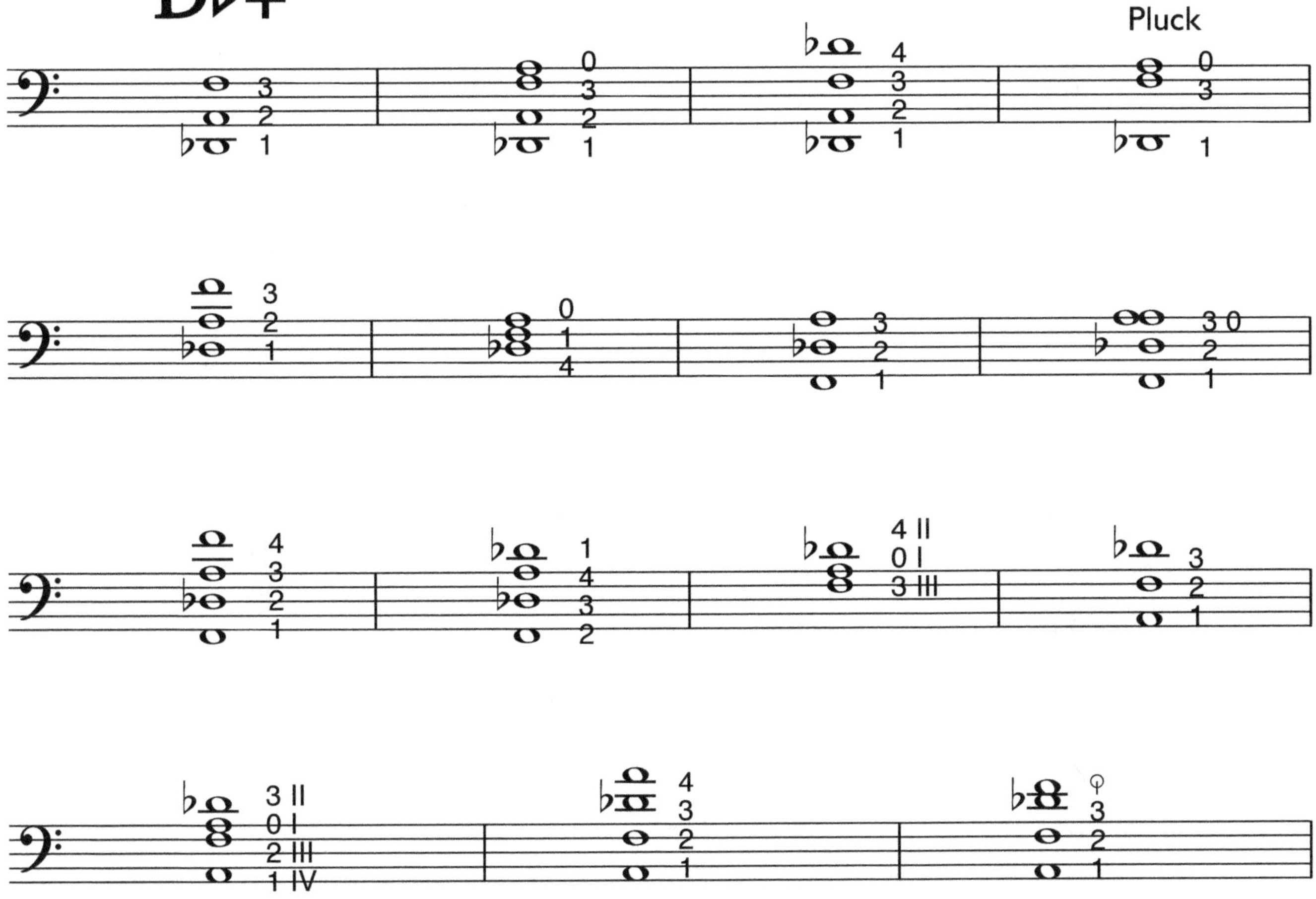

D♭+Δ

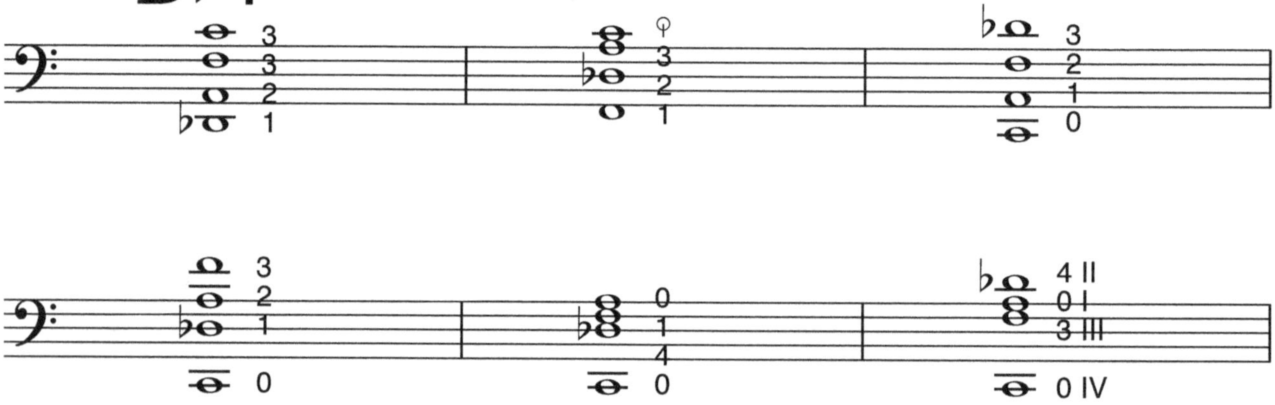

D♭-

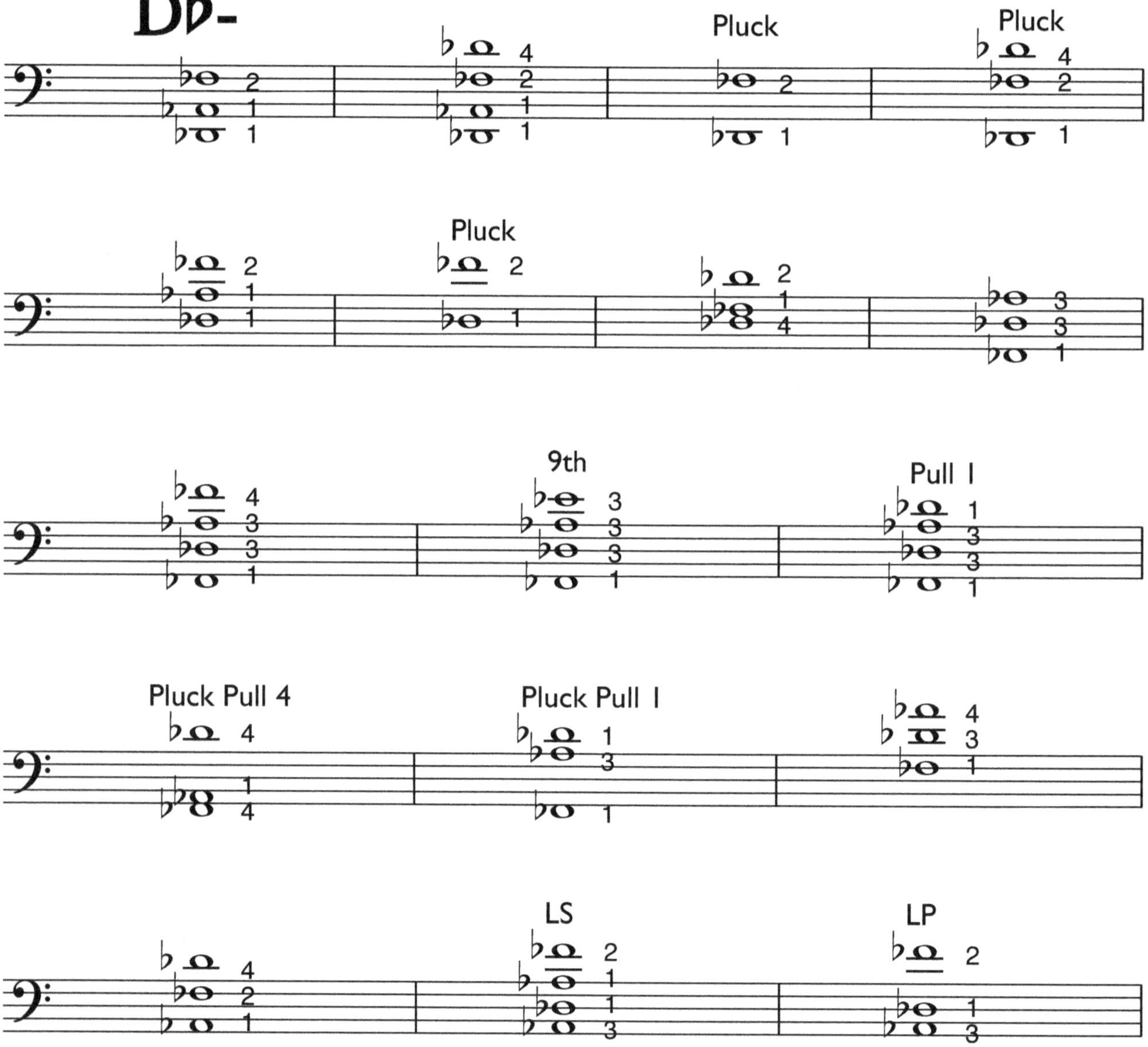

D♭-7

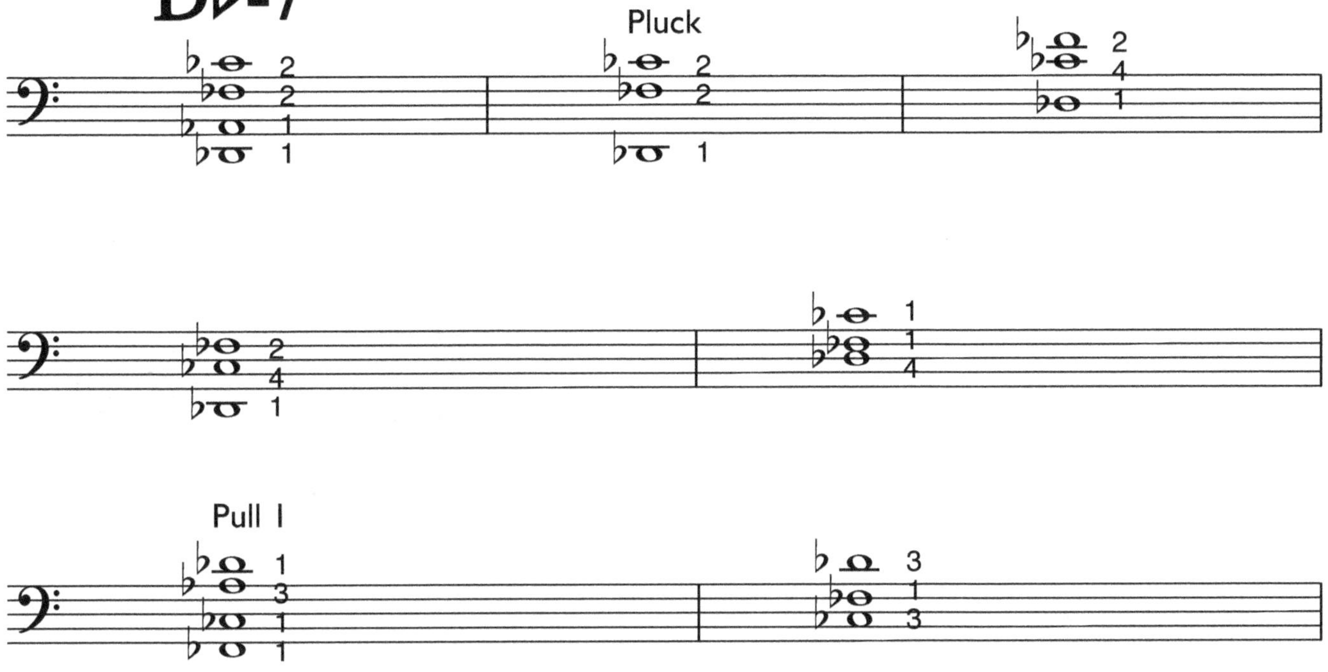

D♭-Δ

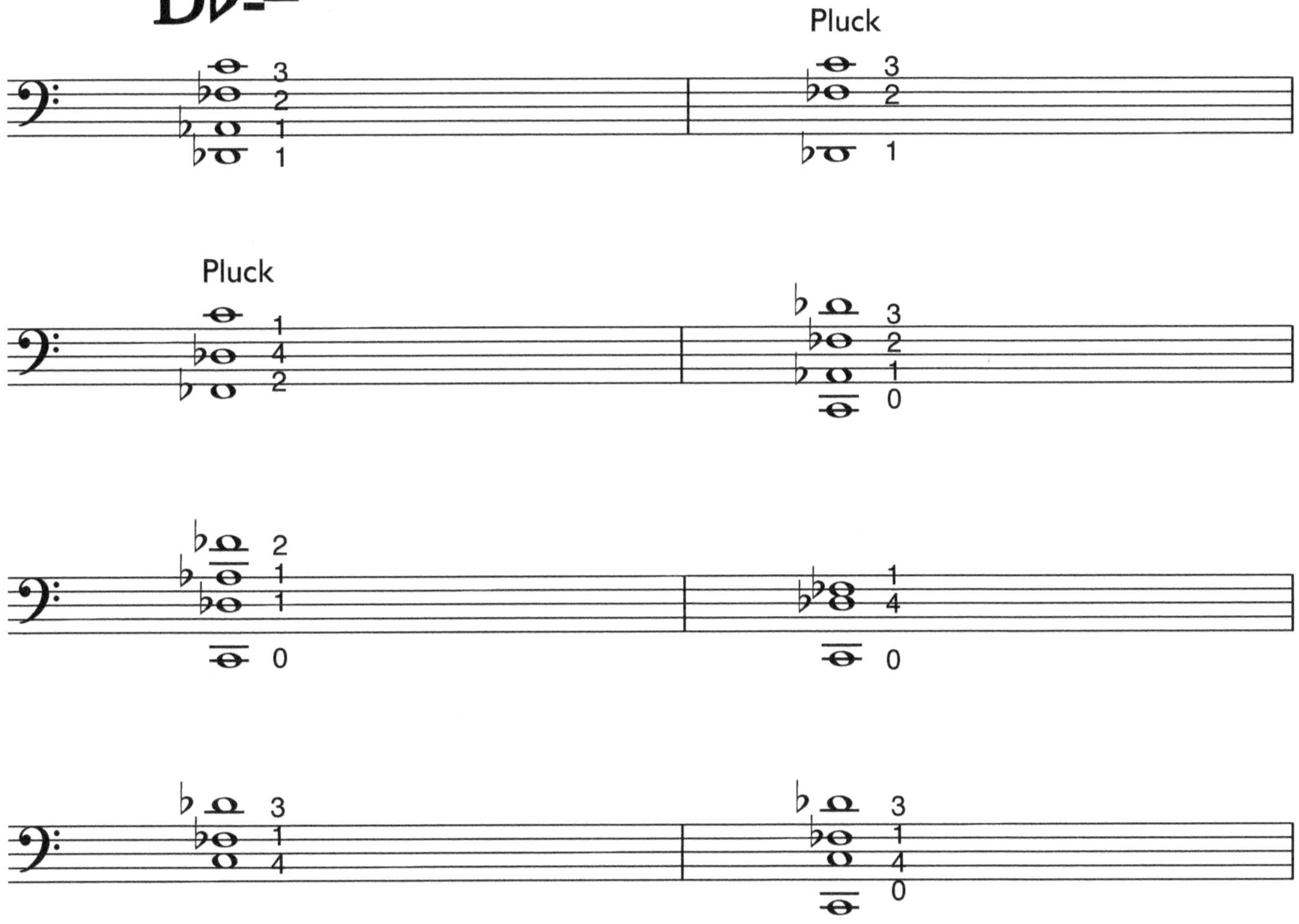

D♭ø7

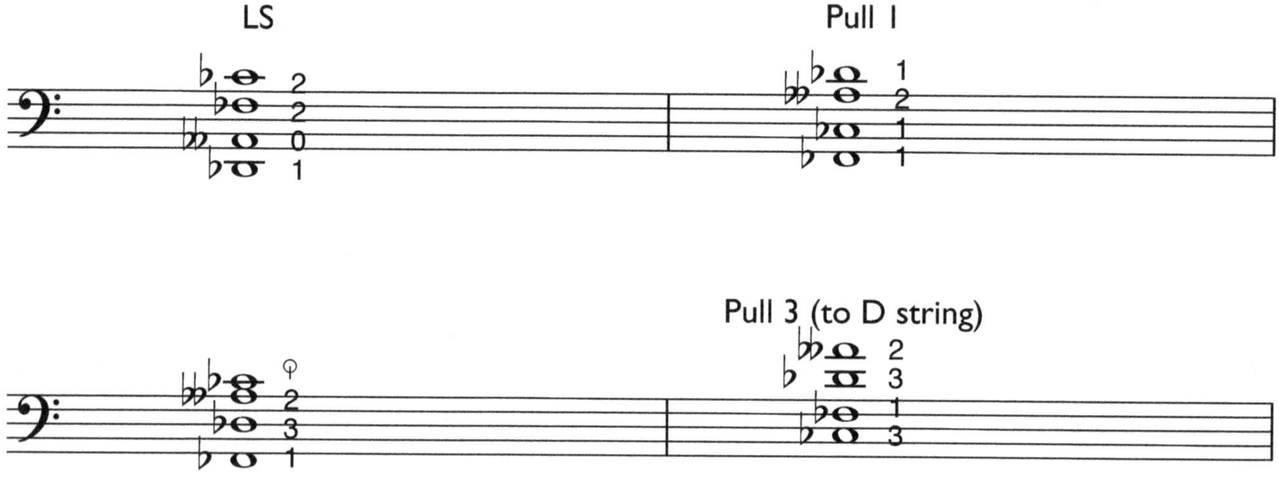
LS
Pull 1
Pull 3 (to D string)

D♭°

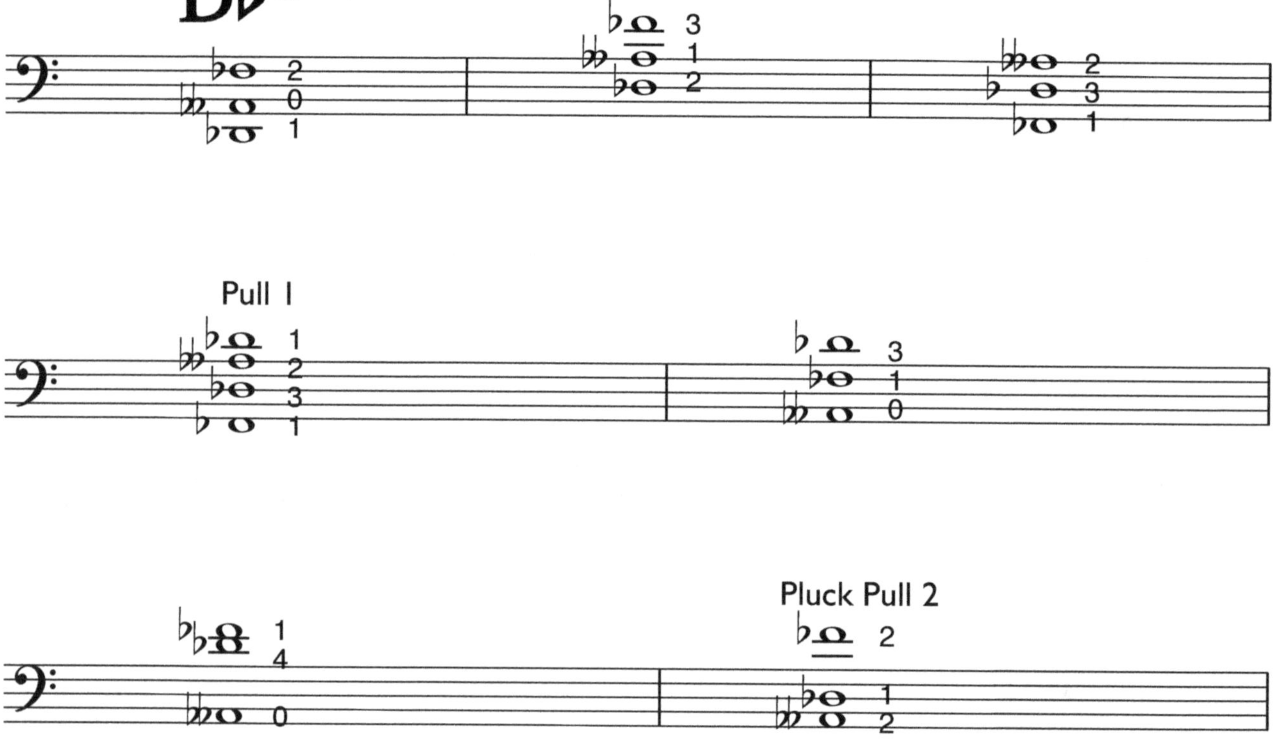
Pull 1
Pluck Pull 2

D♭°7

Pull 1
Pull 2
Pull 2

58

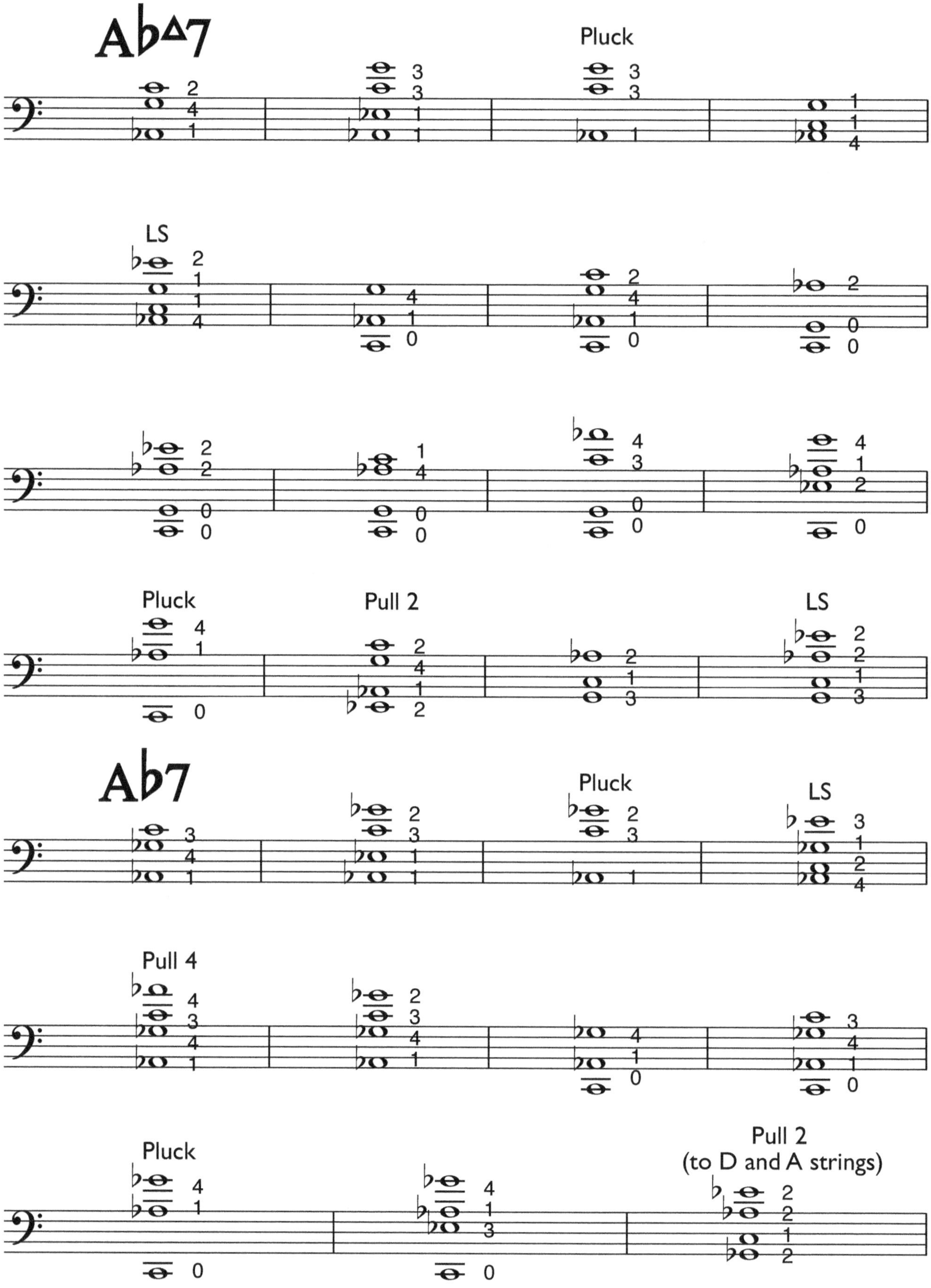
Ab△7
Pluck
LS
Pluck
Pull 2
LS
Ab7
Pluck
LS
Pull 4
Pluck
Pull 2
(to D and A strings)

Ab+

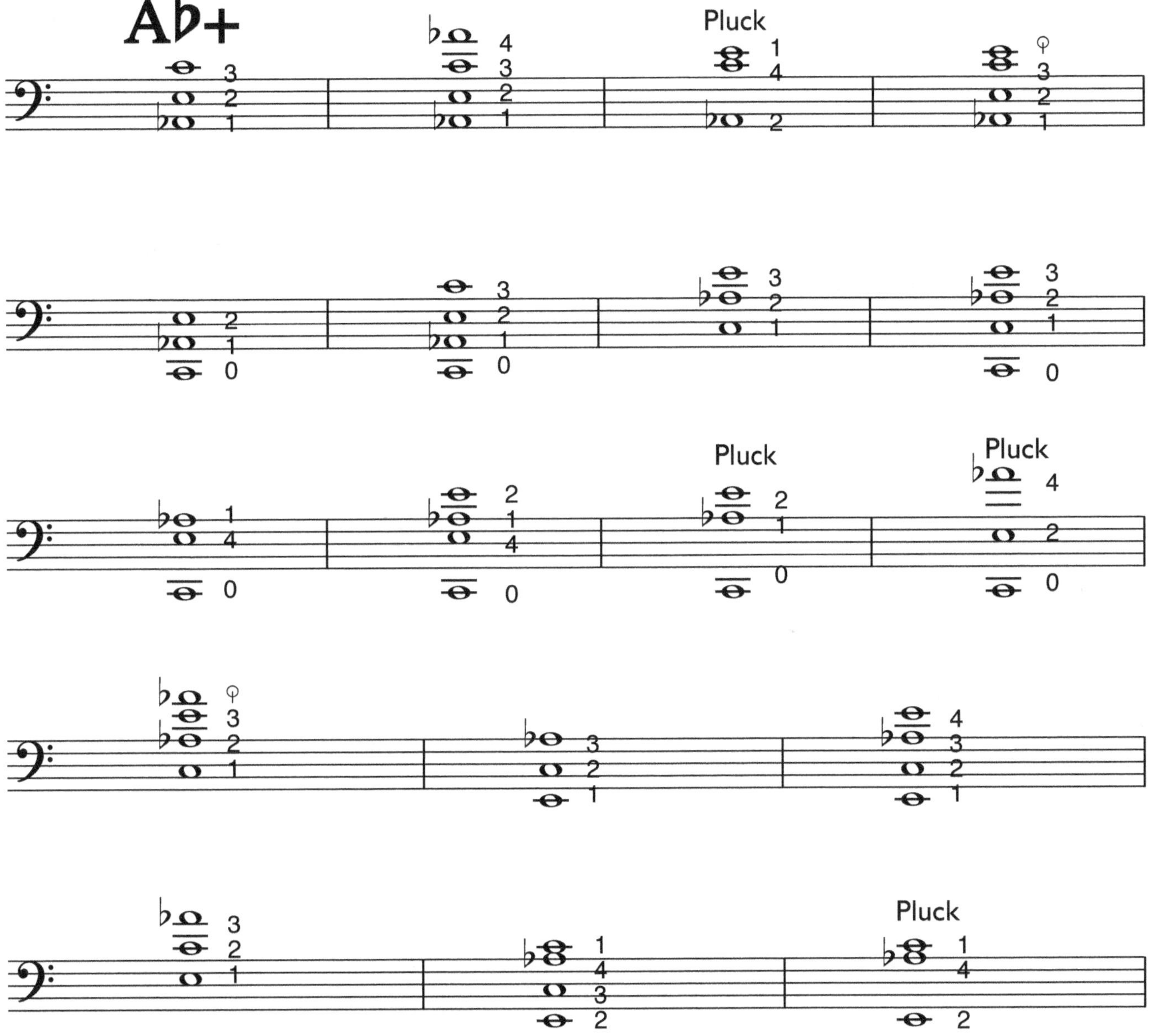

Ab+Δ

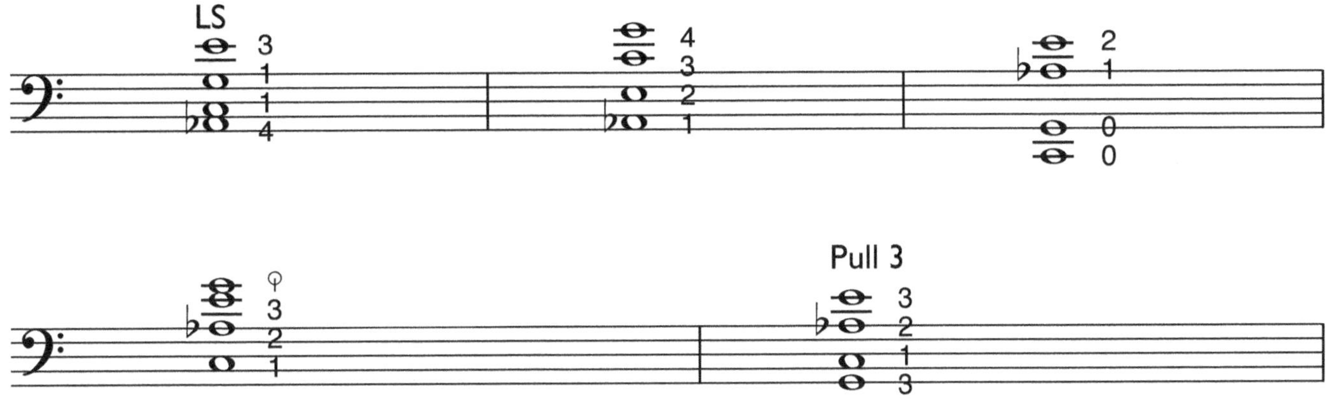

A♭-

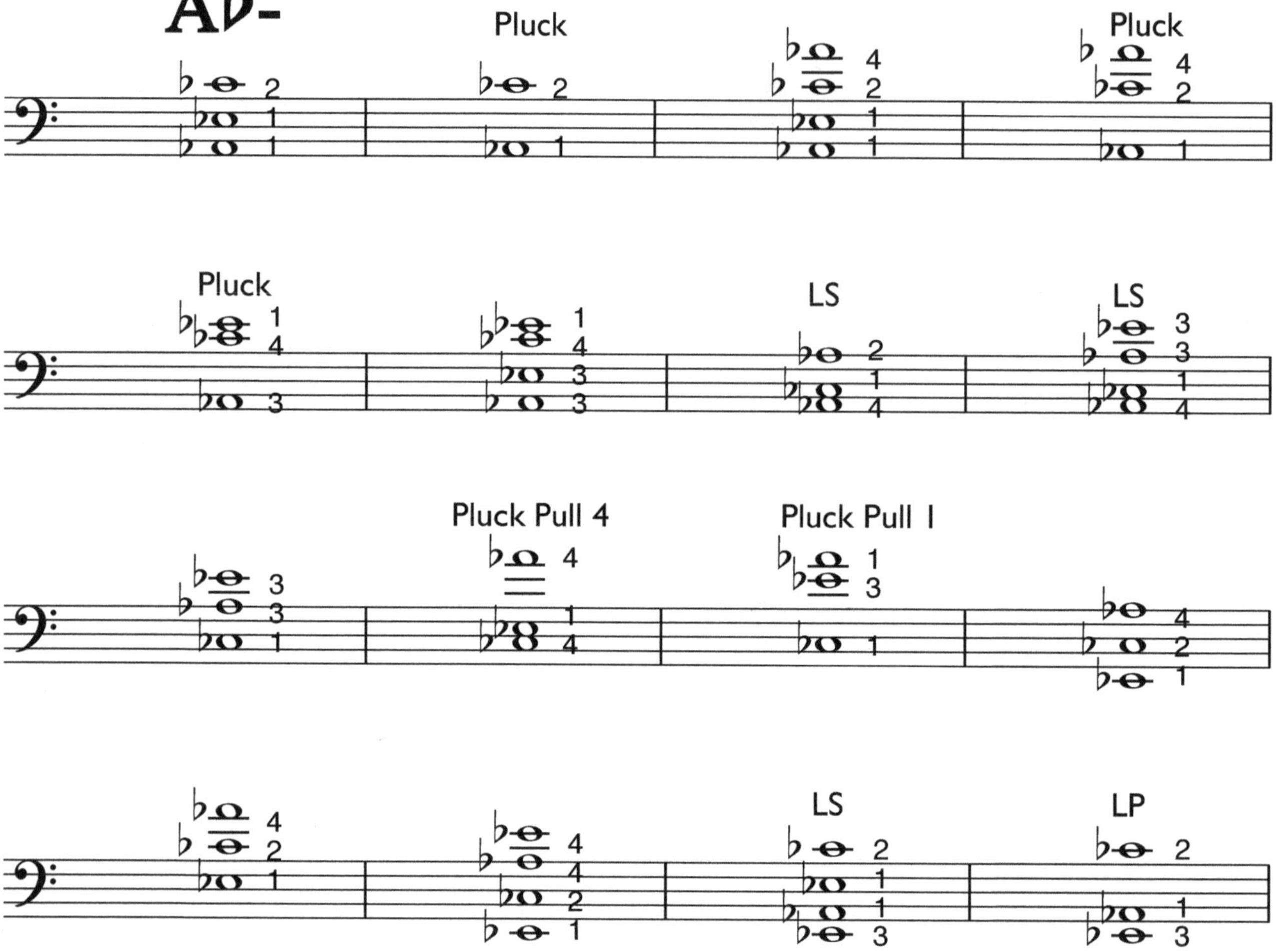
Pluck
Pluck
Pluck
Pluck
LS
LS
Pluck Pull 4
Pluck Pull I
LS
LP

A♭-7

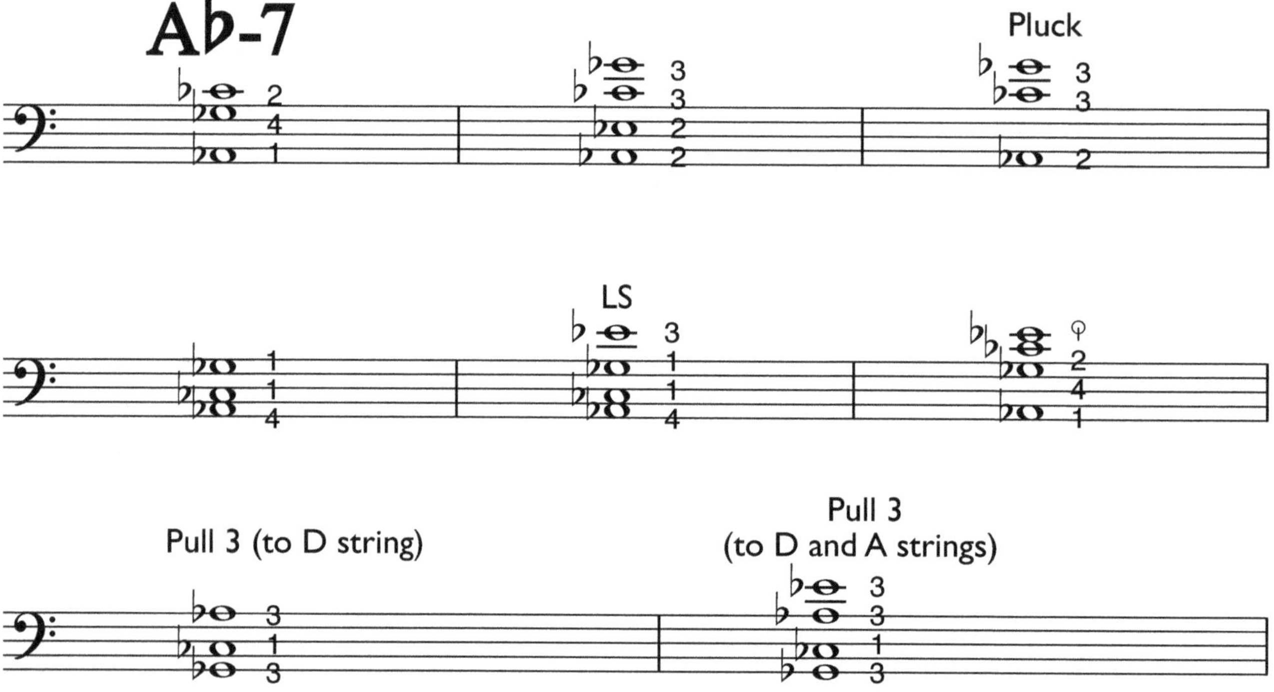
Pluck
LS
Pull 3 (to D string)
Pull 3
(to D and A strings)

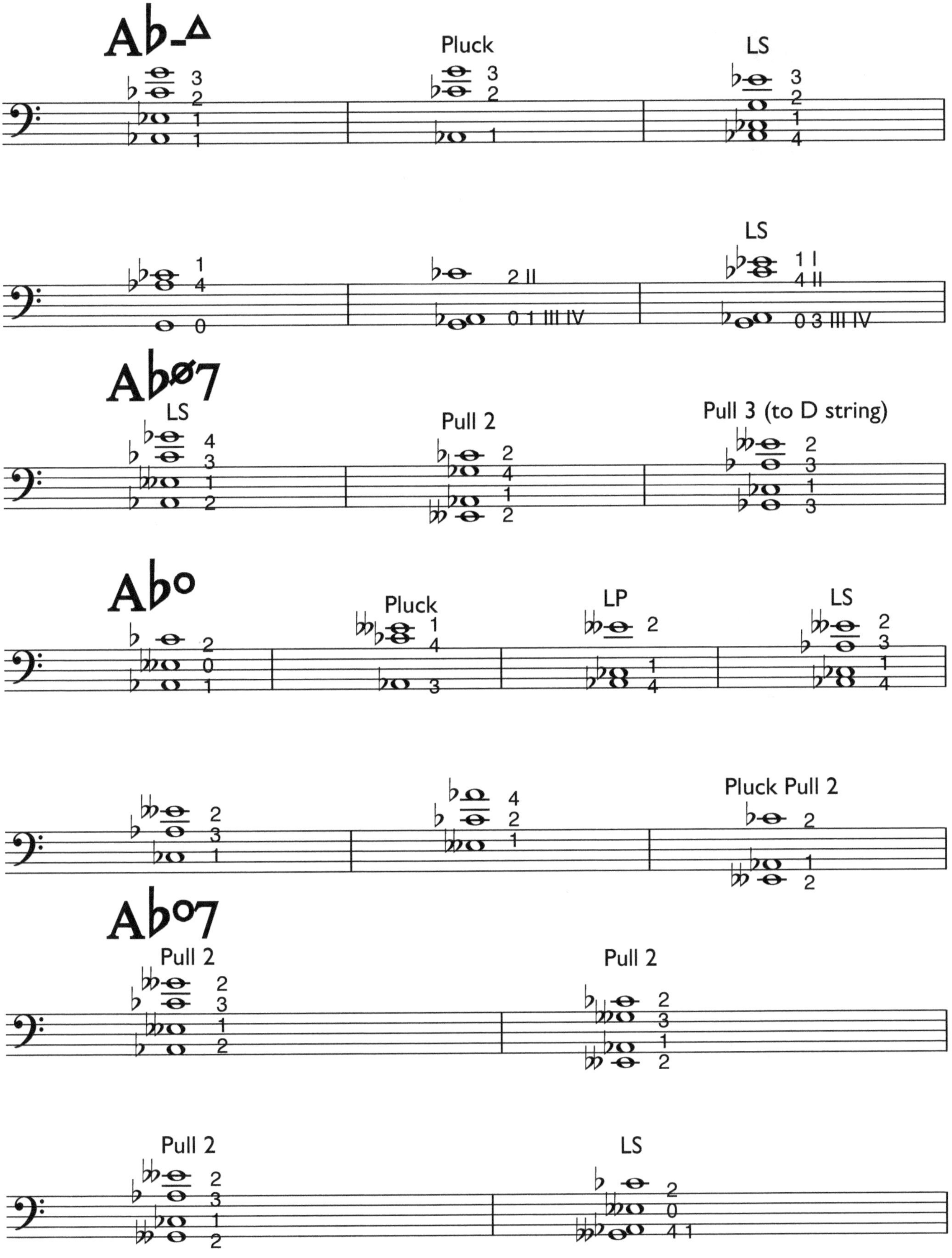
Ab-Δ
Pluck
LS
LS
Abø7
LS
Pull 2
Pull 3 (to D string)
Abo
Pluck
LP
LS
Pluck Pull 2
Abo7
Pull 2
Pull 2
Pull 2
LS

E♭

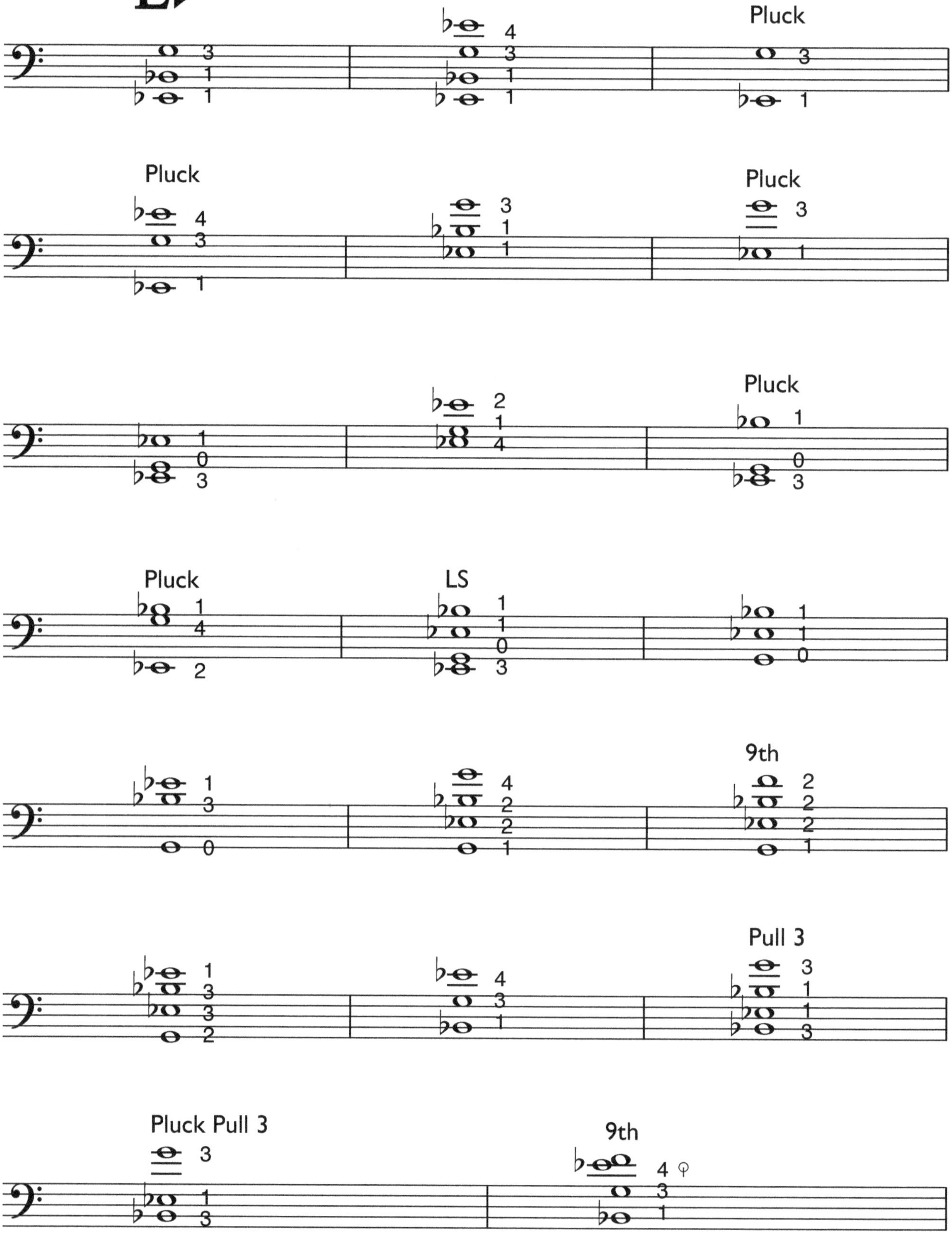

E♭△7

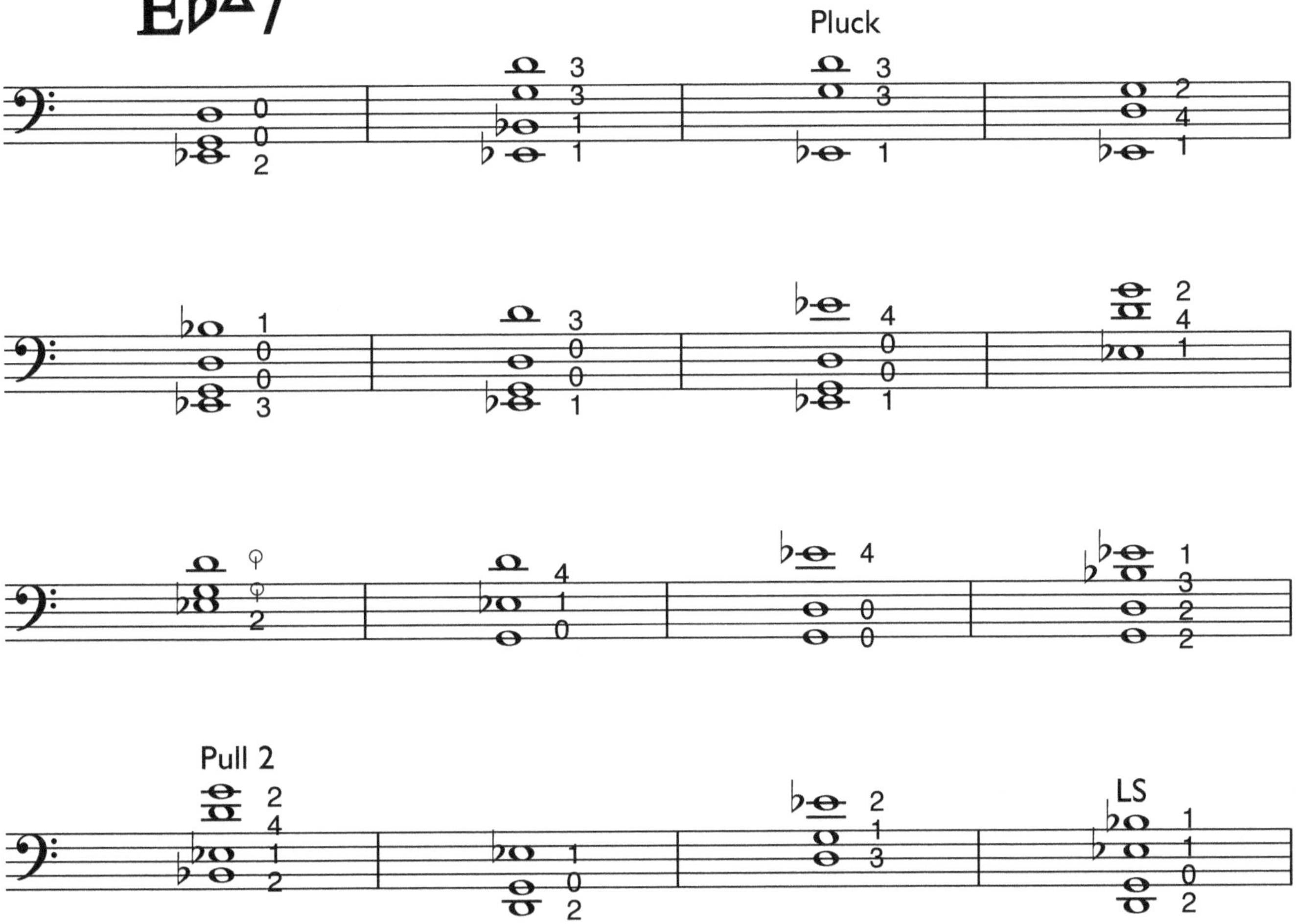
Pluck
Pull 2
LS

E♭7

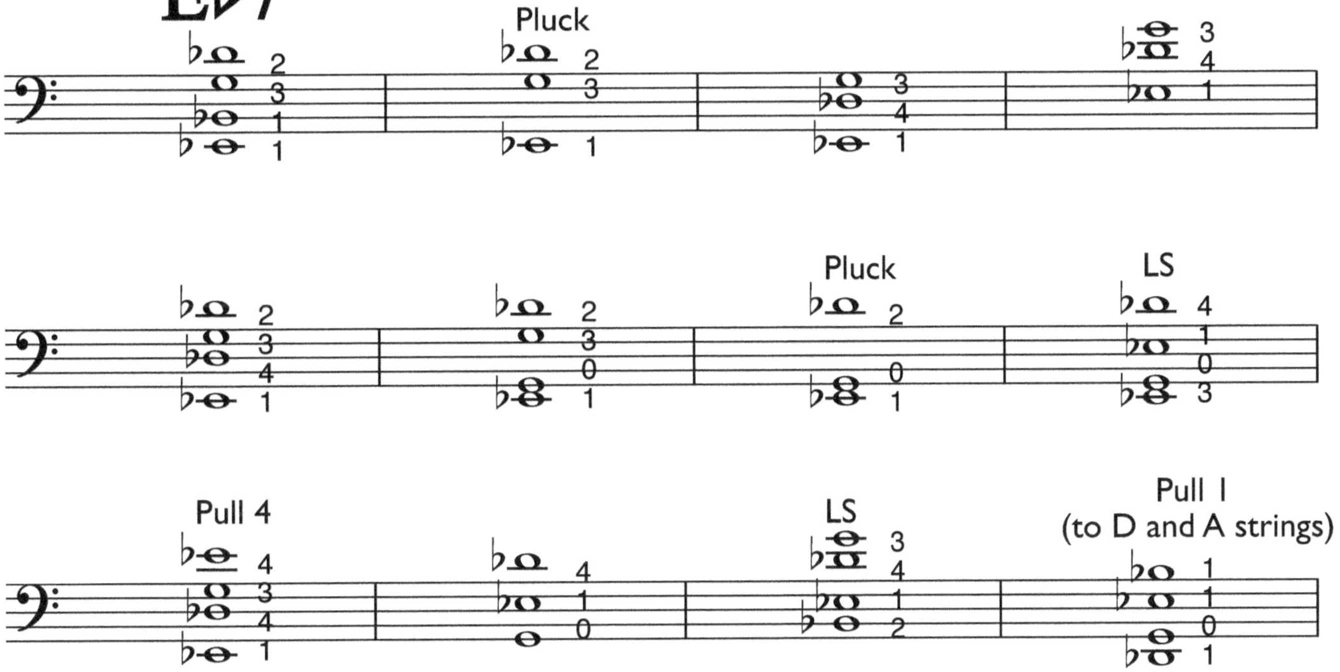
Pluck
Pluck
LS
Pull 4
LS
Pull 1
(to D and A strings)

E♭+

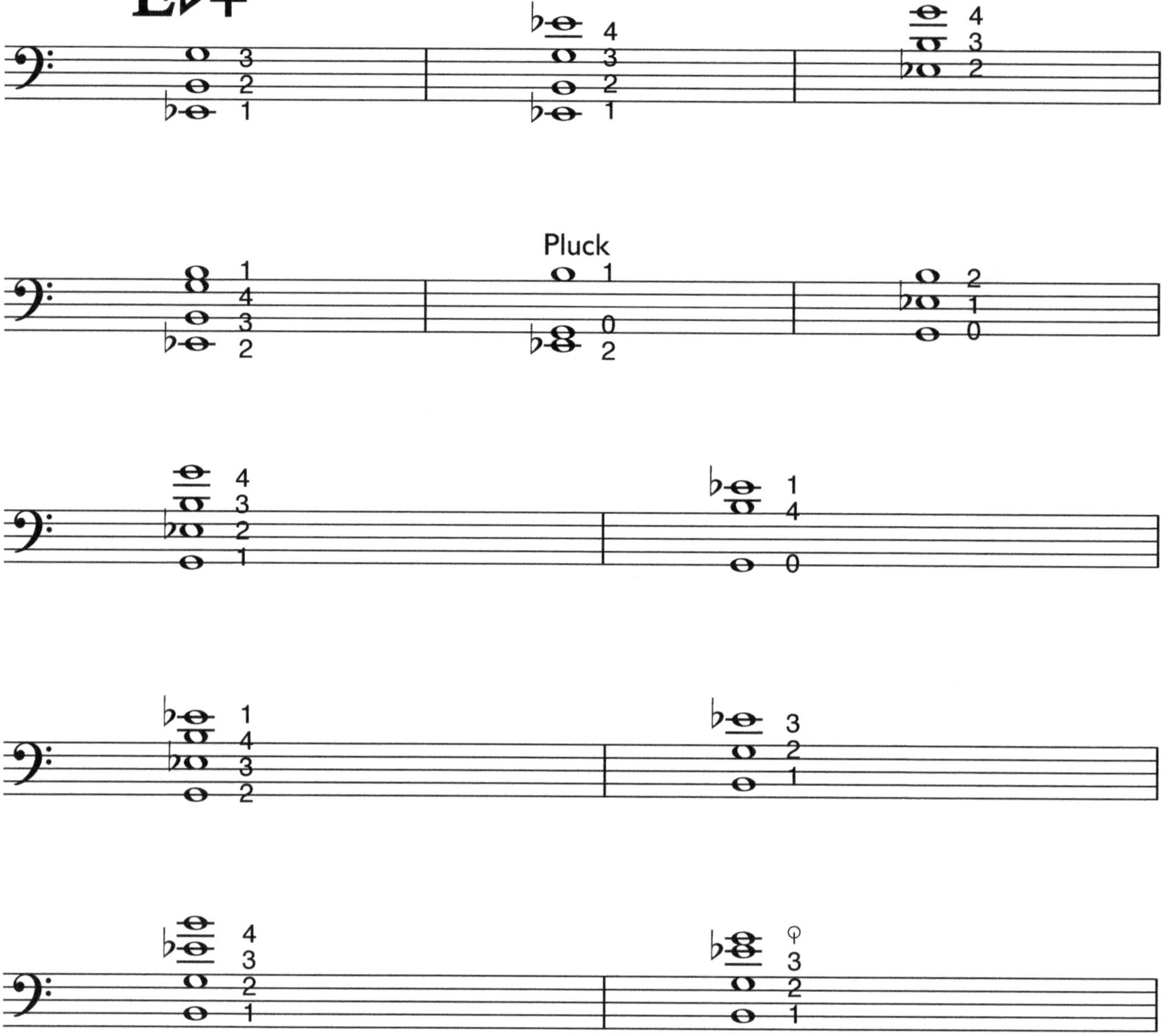

E♭+Δ

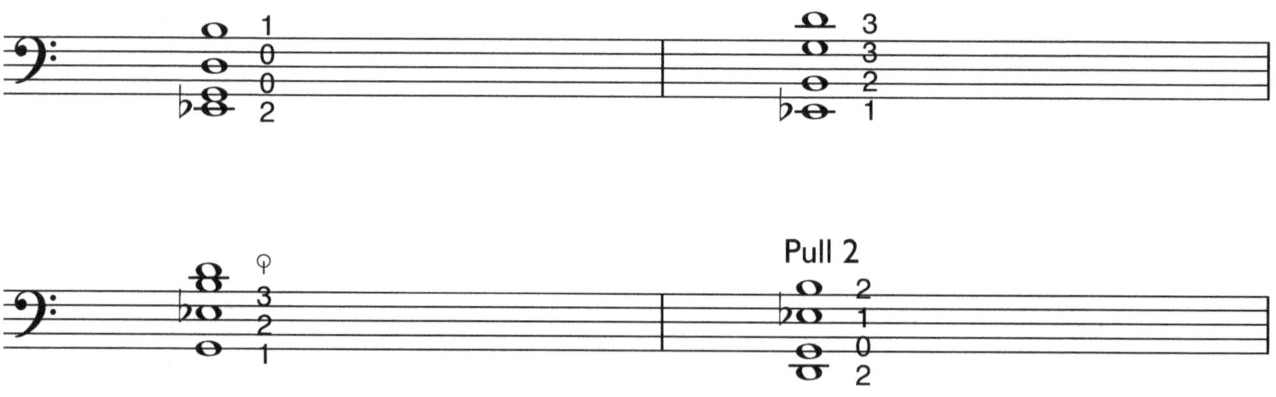

Eb-

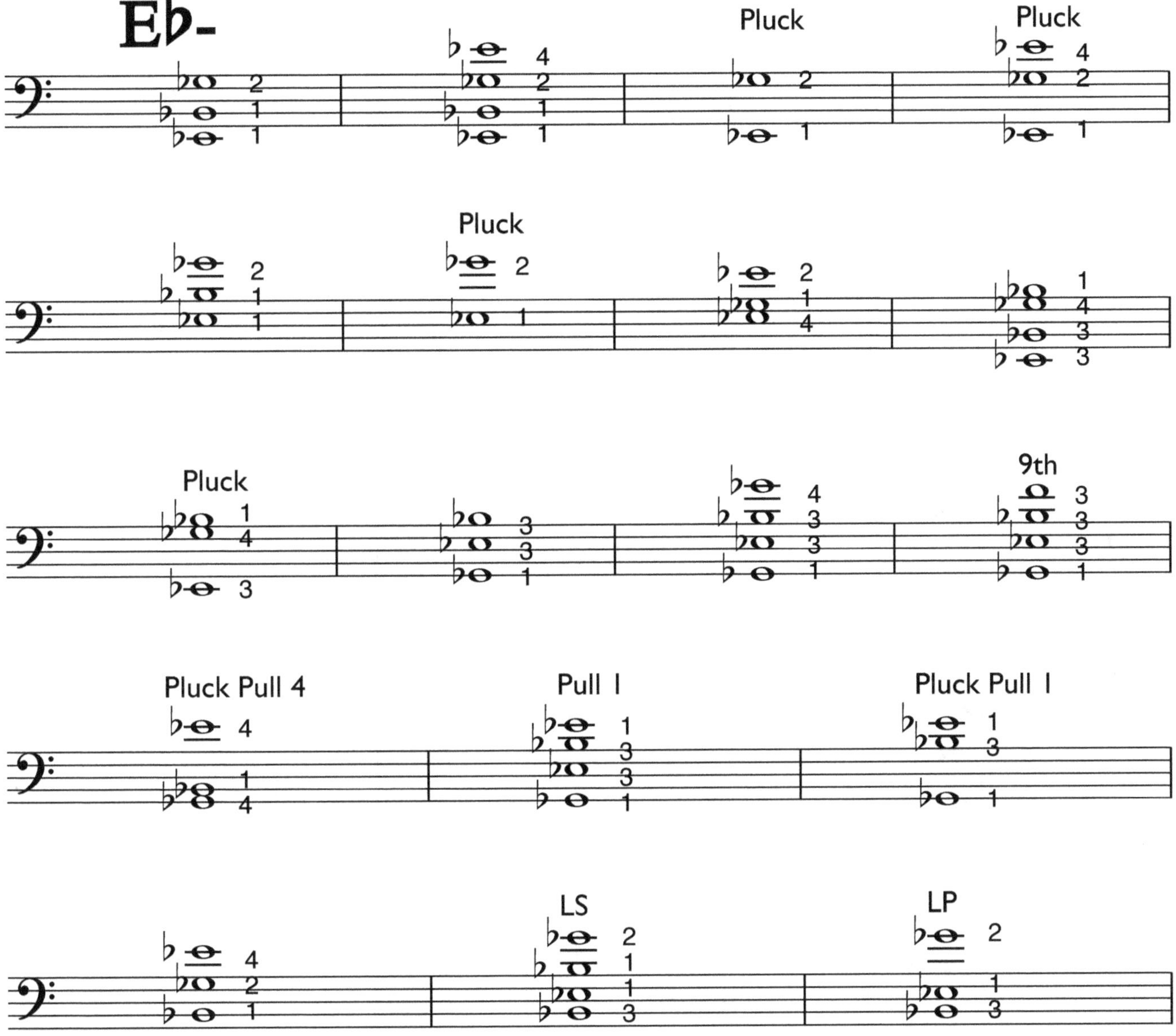
Pluck
Pluck
Pluck
Pluck
9th
Pluck Pull 4
Pull I
Pluck Pull I
LS
LP

Eb-7

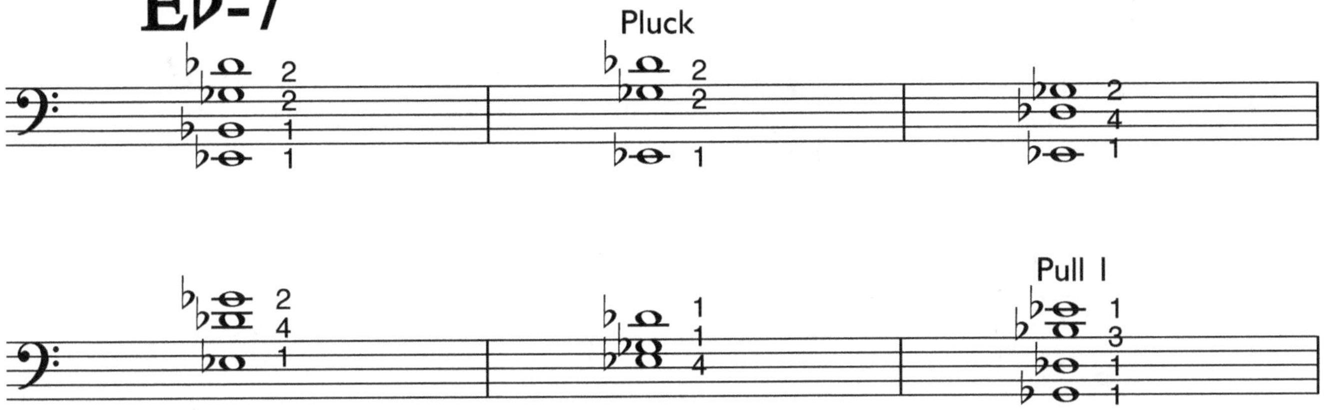
Pluck
Pull I

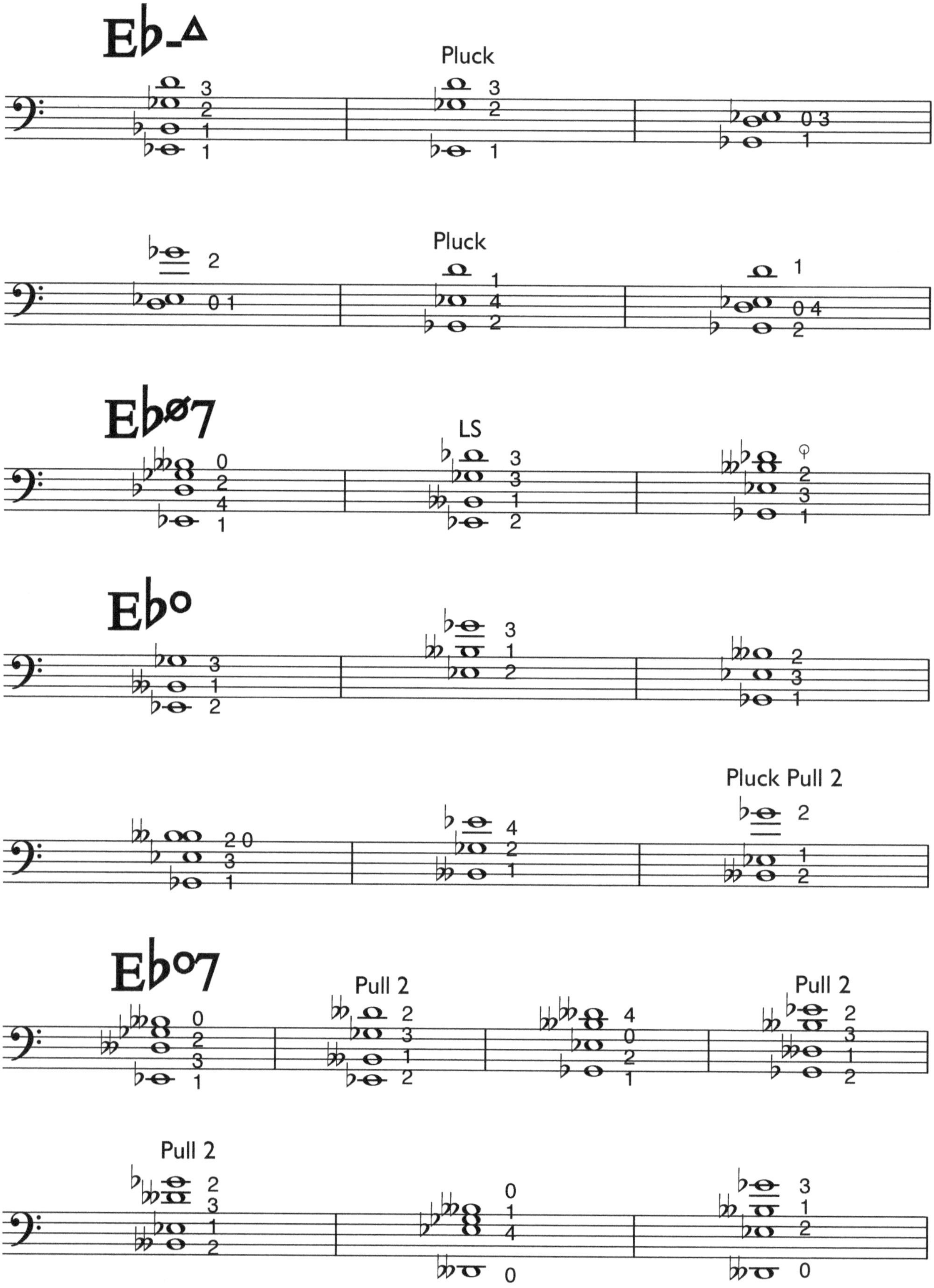
Eb-Δ
Pluck
Pluck
Eb∅7
LS
Eb°
Pluck Pull 2
Eb°7
Pull 2
Pull 2
Pull 2

68

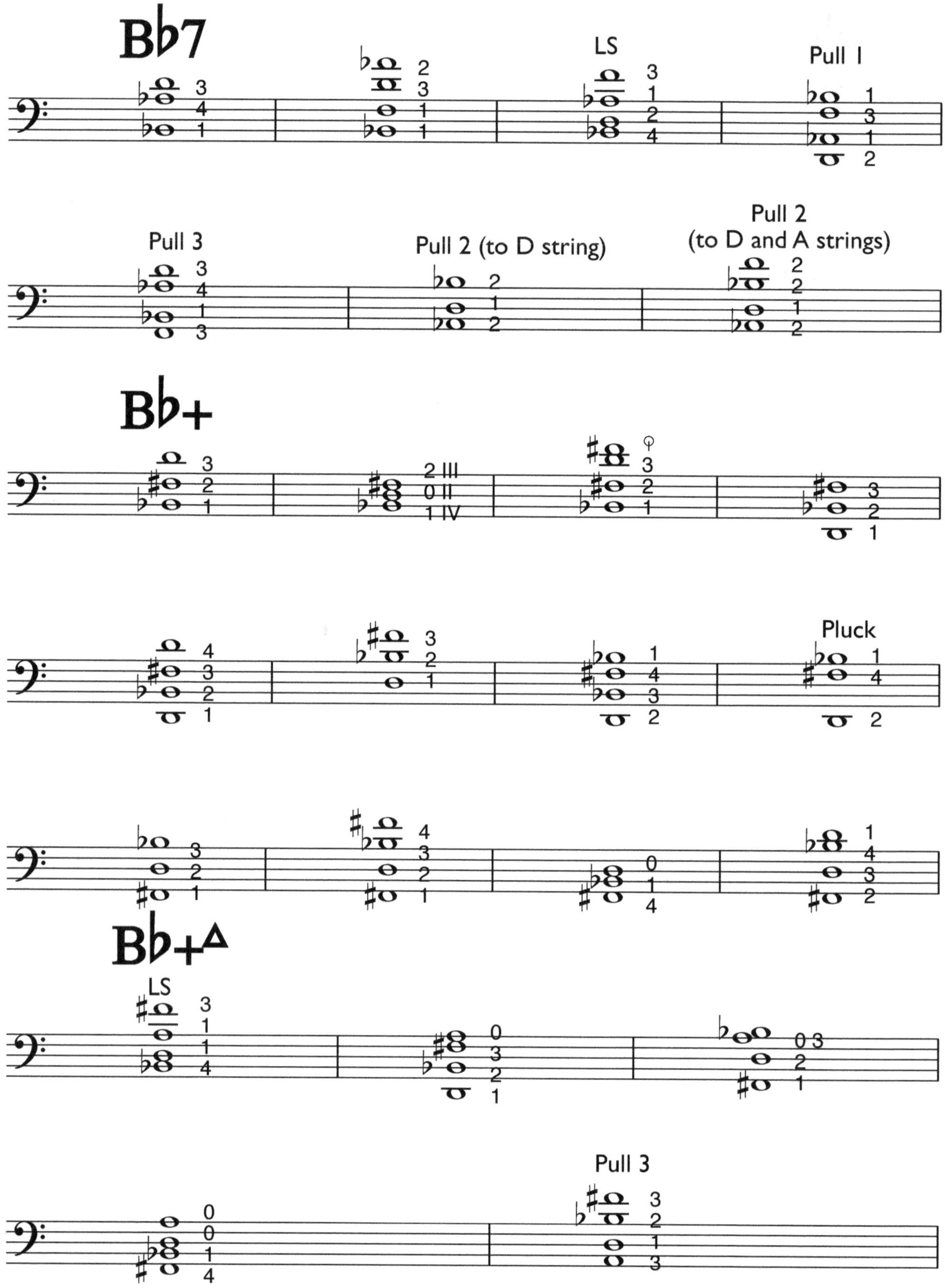
Bb7
LS
Pull 1
Pull 3
Pull 2 (to D string)
Pull 2
(to D and A strings)
Bb+
Pluck
Bb+Δ
LS
Pull 3

Bb-

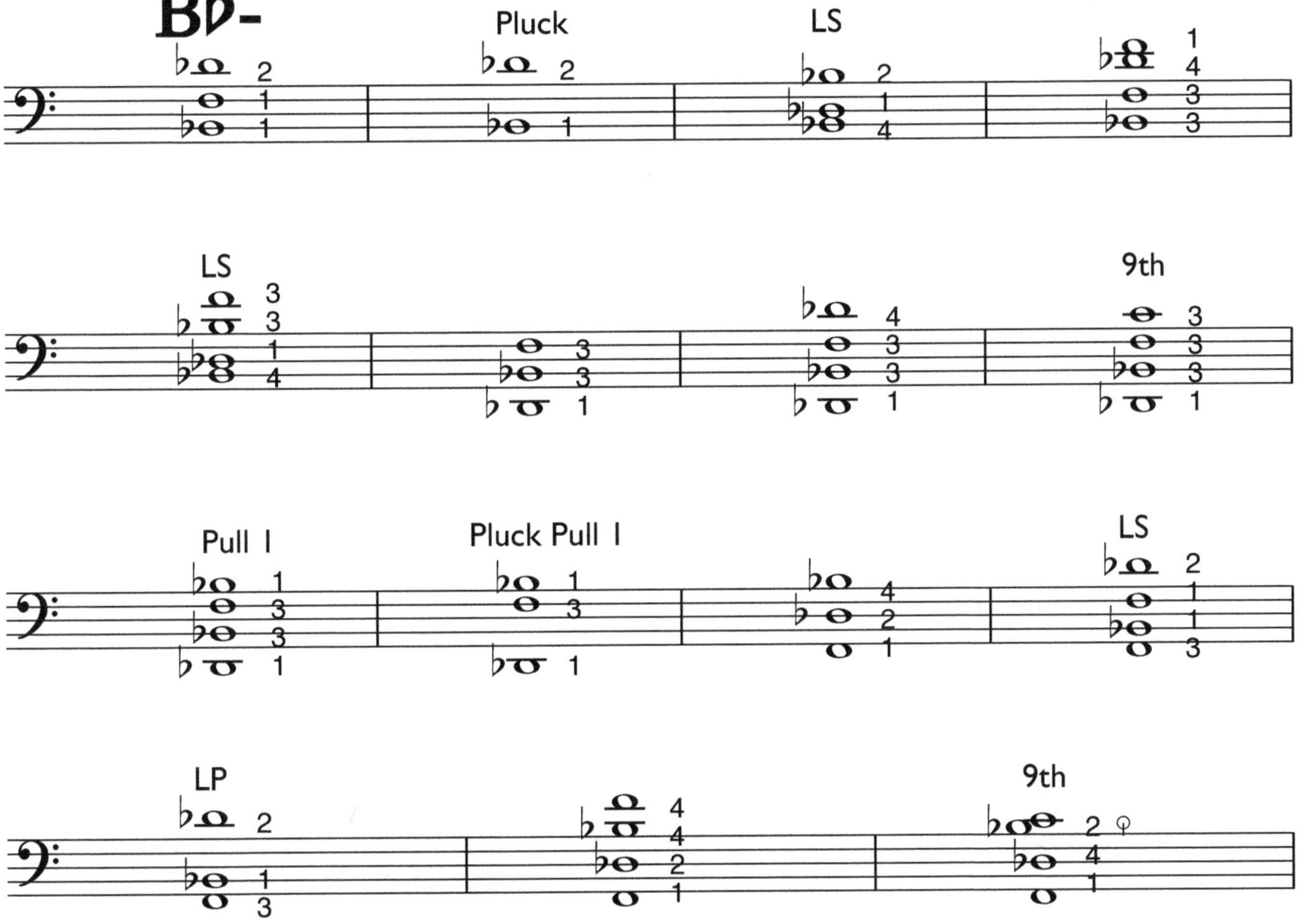
Pluck
LS
LS
9th
Pull 1
Pluck Pull 1
LS
LP
9th

Bb-7

LS
Pull 1
LS
Pull 3 (to D string)
Pull 3
(to D and A strings)

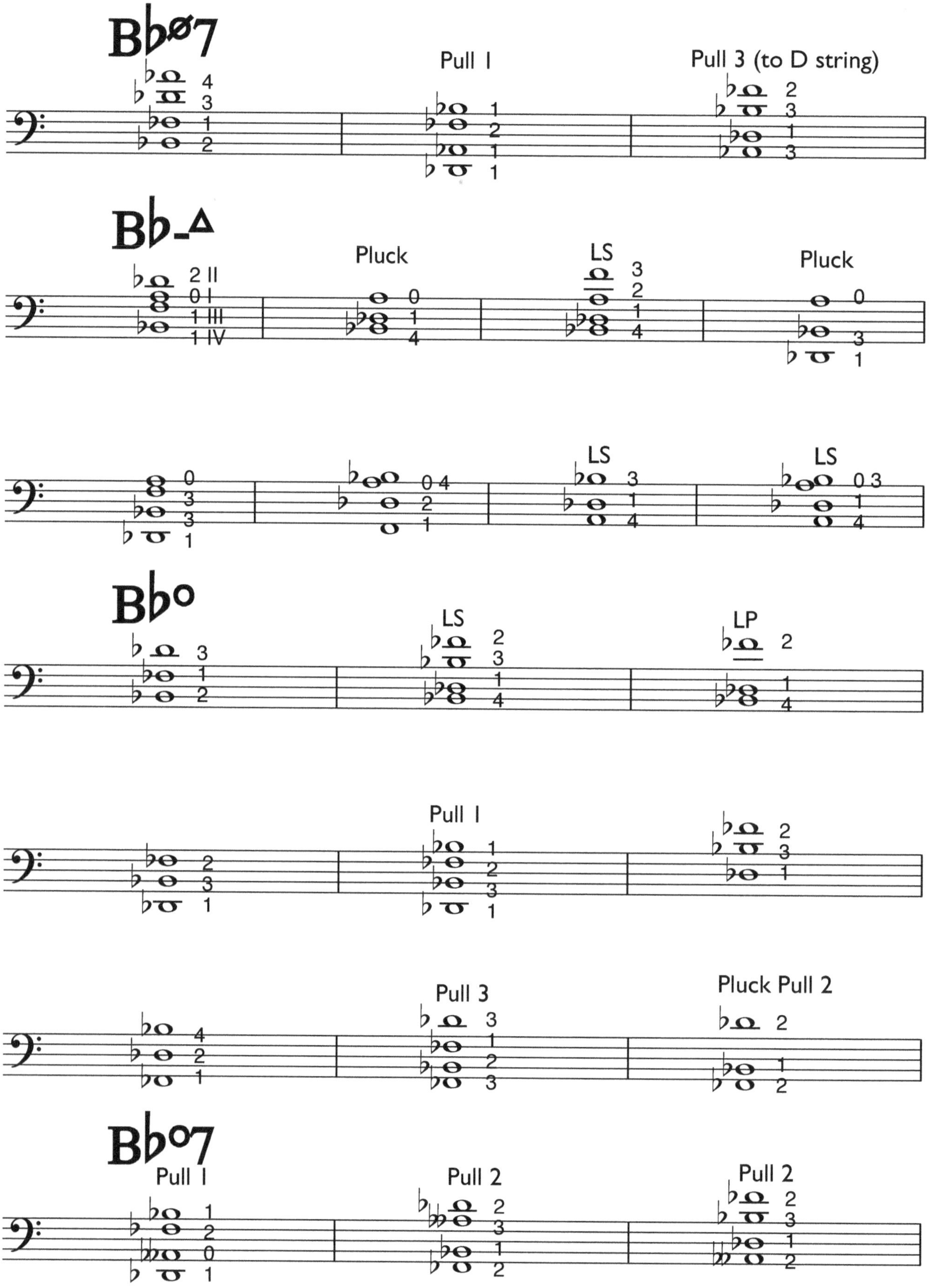
Bbø7
Pull 1
Pull 3 (to D string)
Bb-△
Pluck
LS
Pluck
LS
LS
Bbo
LS
LP
Pull 1
Pull 3
Pluck Pull 2
Bbo7
Pull 1
Pull 2
Pull 2

F

73

F+

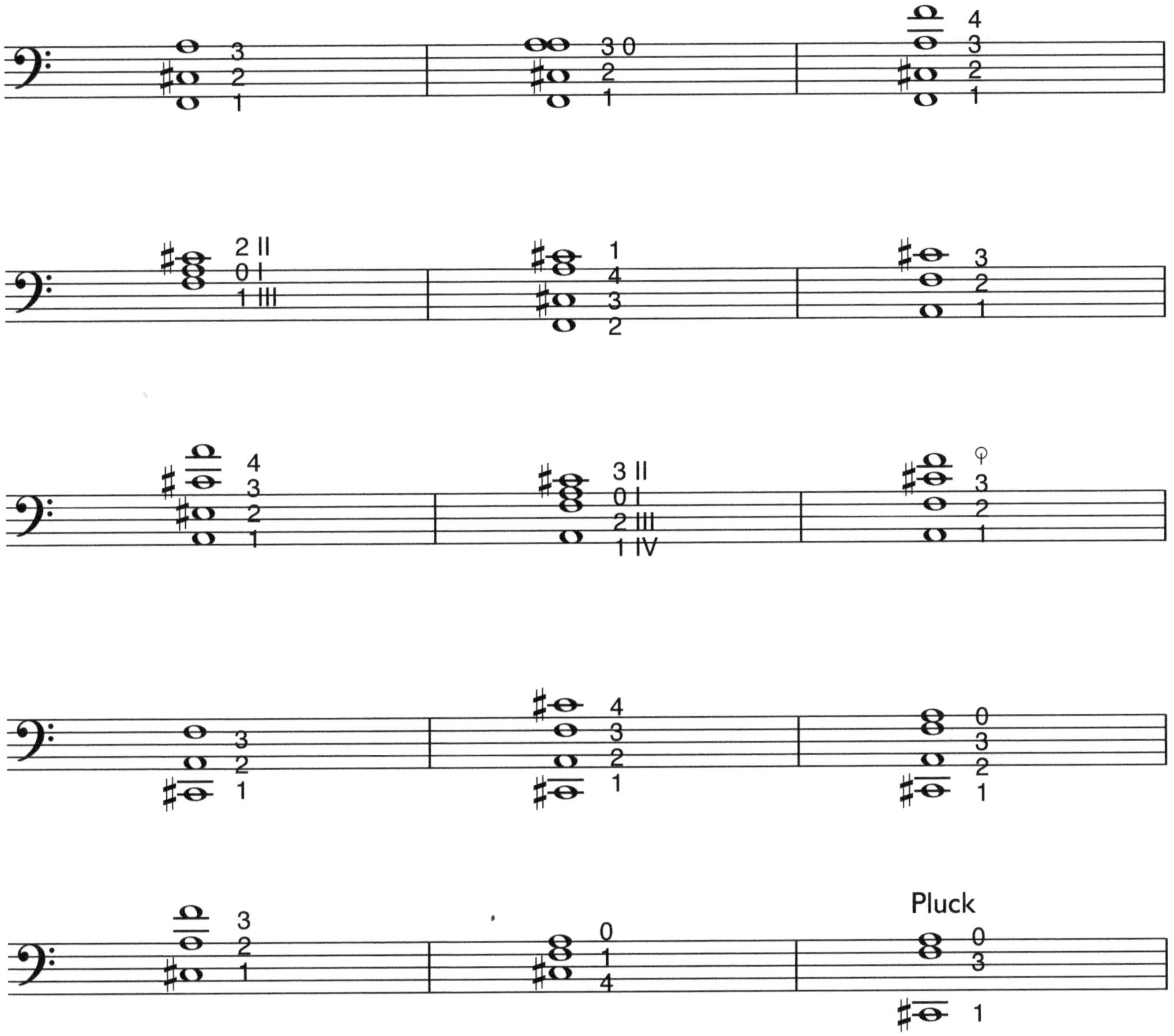

F+$^{\Delta}$

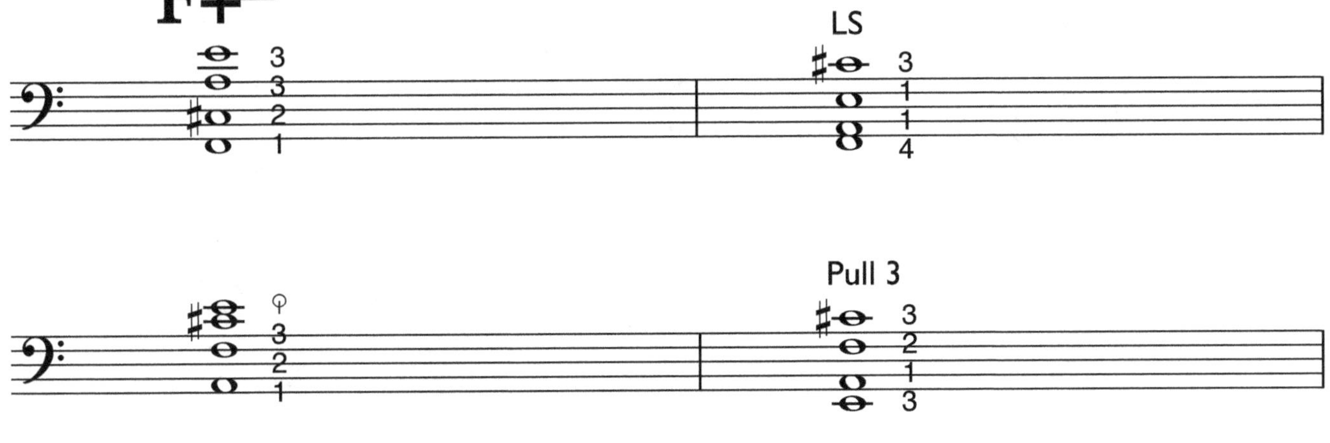

F-

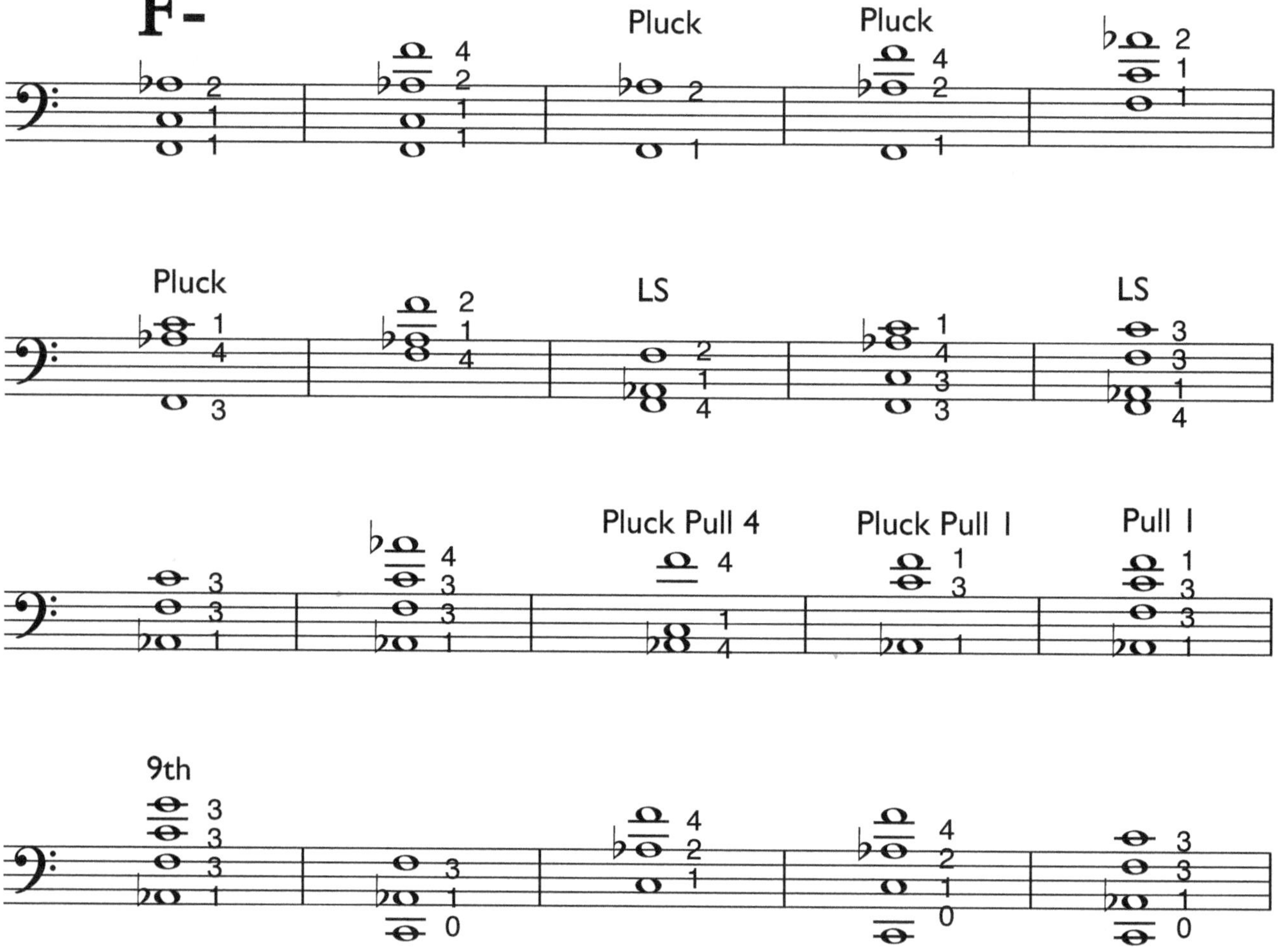
Pluck
Pluck
Pluck
LS
LS
Pluck Pull 4
Pluck Pull 1
Pull 1
9th

F-7

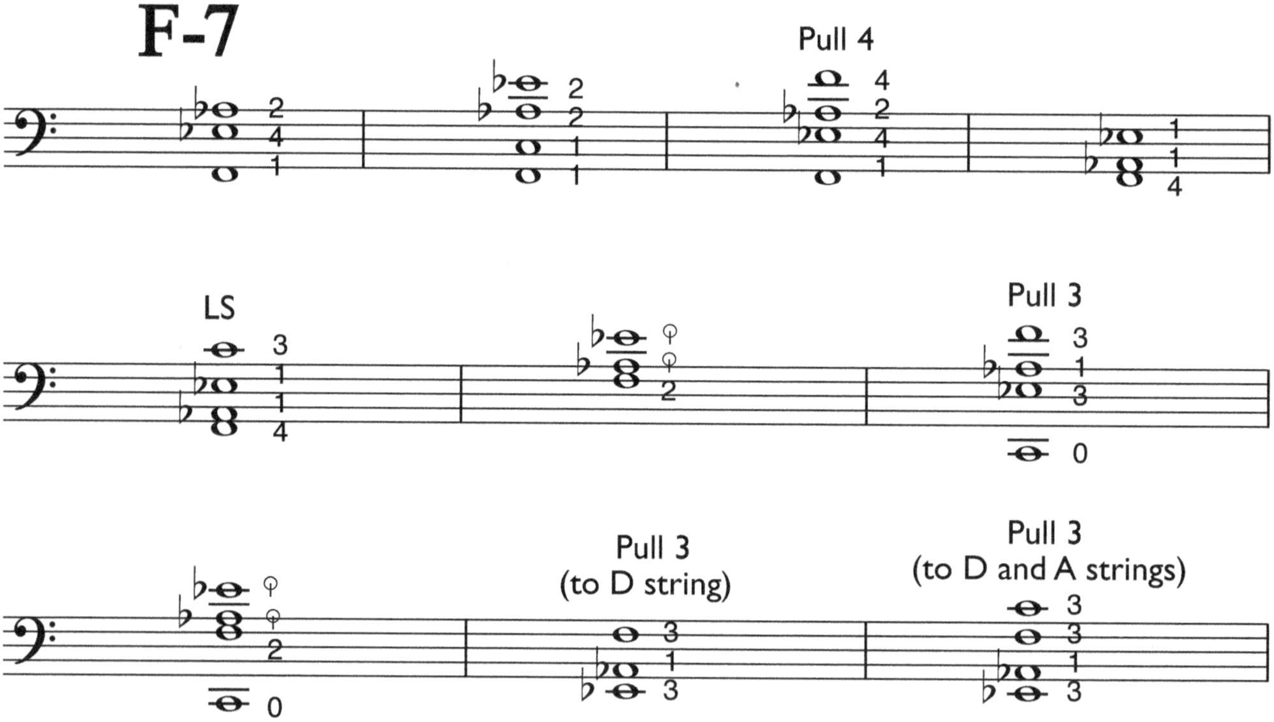
Pull 4
LS
Pull 3
Pull 3
(to D string)
Pull 3
(to D and A strings)

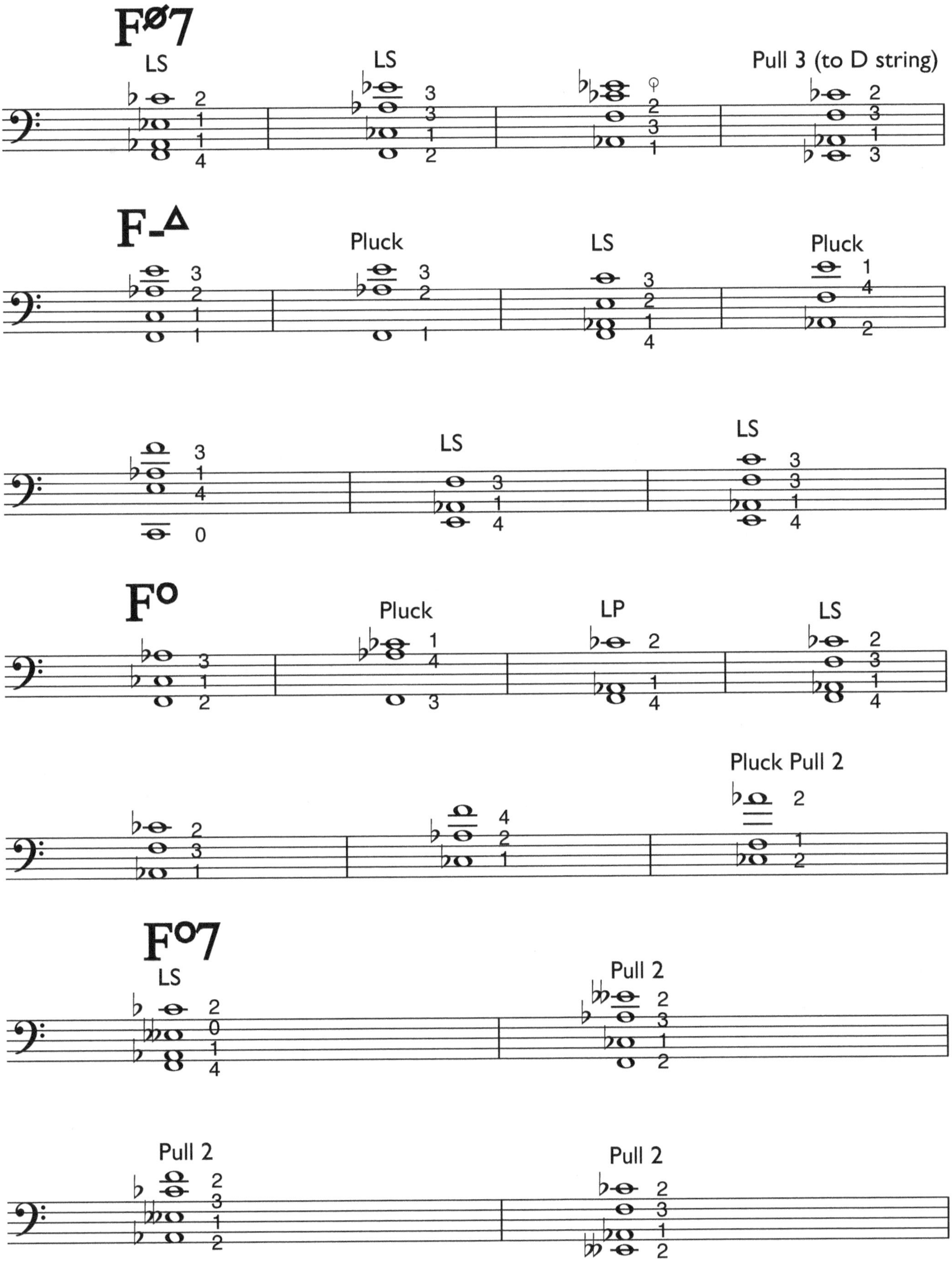
Fø7
LS
LS
Pull 3 (to D string)
F-Δ
Pluck
LS
Pluck
LS
LS
F°
Pluck
LP
LS
Pluck Pull 2
F°7
LS
Pull 2
Pull 2
Pull 2

Bonus
Section

An Introduction to Extended Chords

C

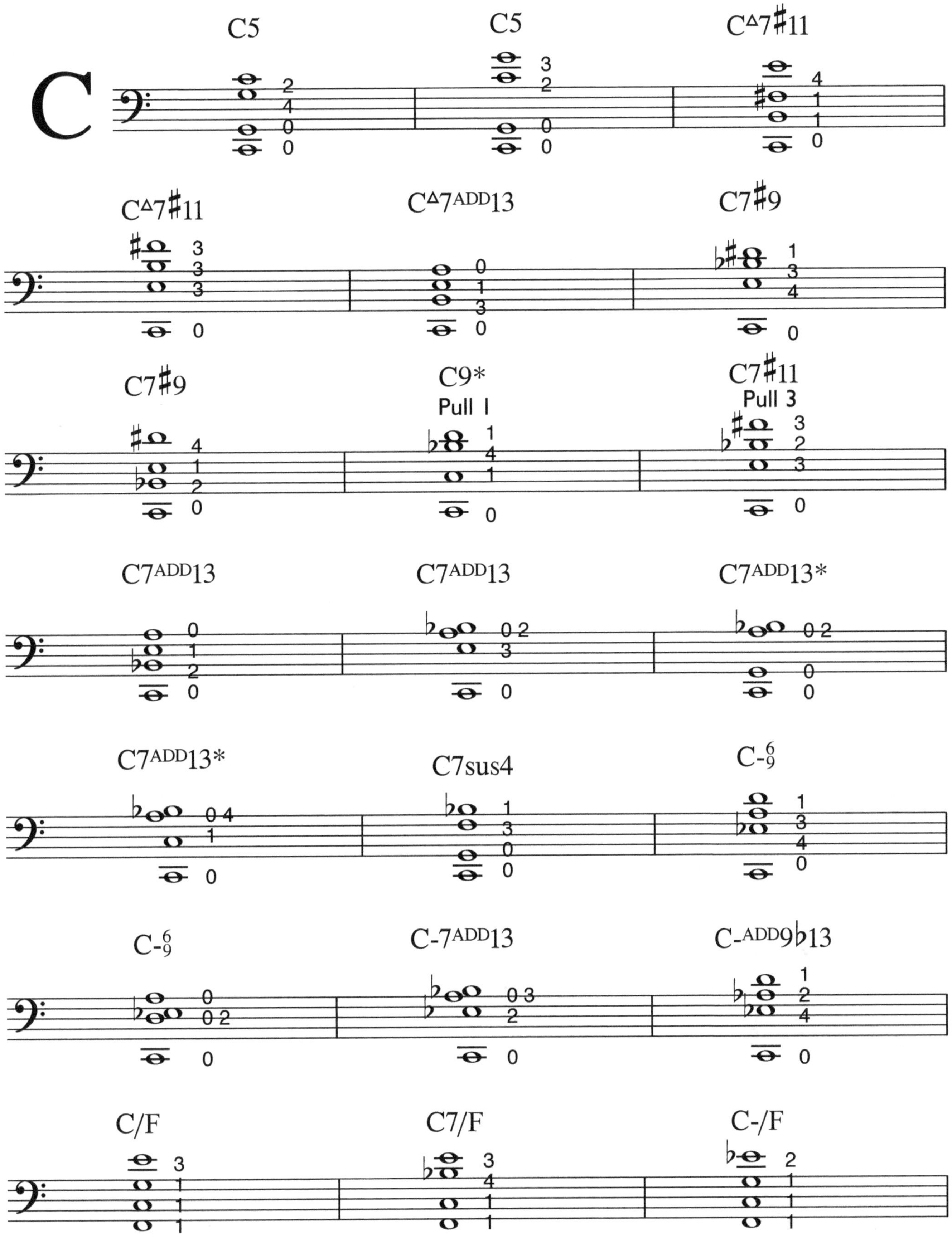
C5
C5
CΔ7#11
CΔ7#11
CΔ7ADD13
C7#9
C7#9
C9*
Pull 1
C7#11
Pull 3
C7ADD13
C7ADD13
C7ADD13*
C7ADD13*
C7sus4
C-6/9
C-6/9
C-7ADD13
C-ADD9♭13
C/F
C7/F
C-/F

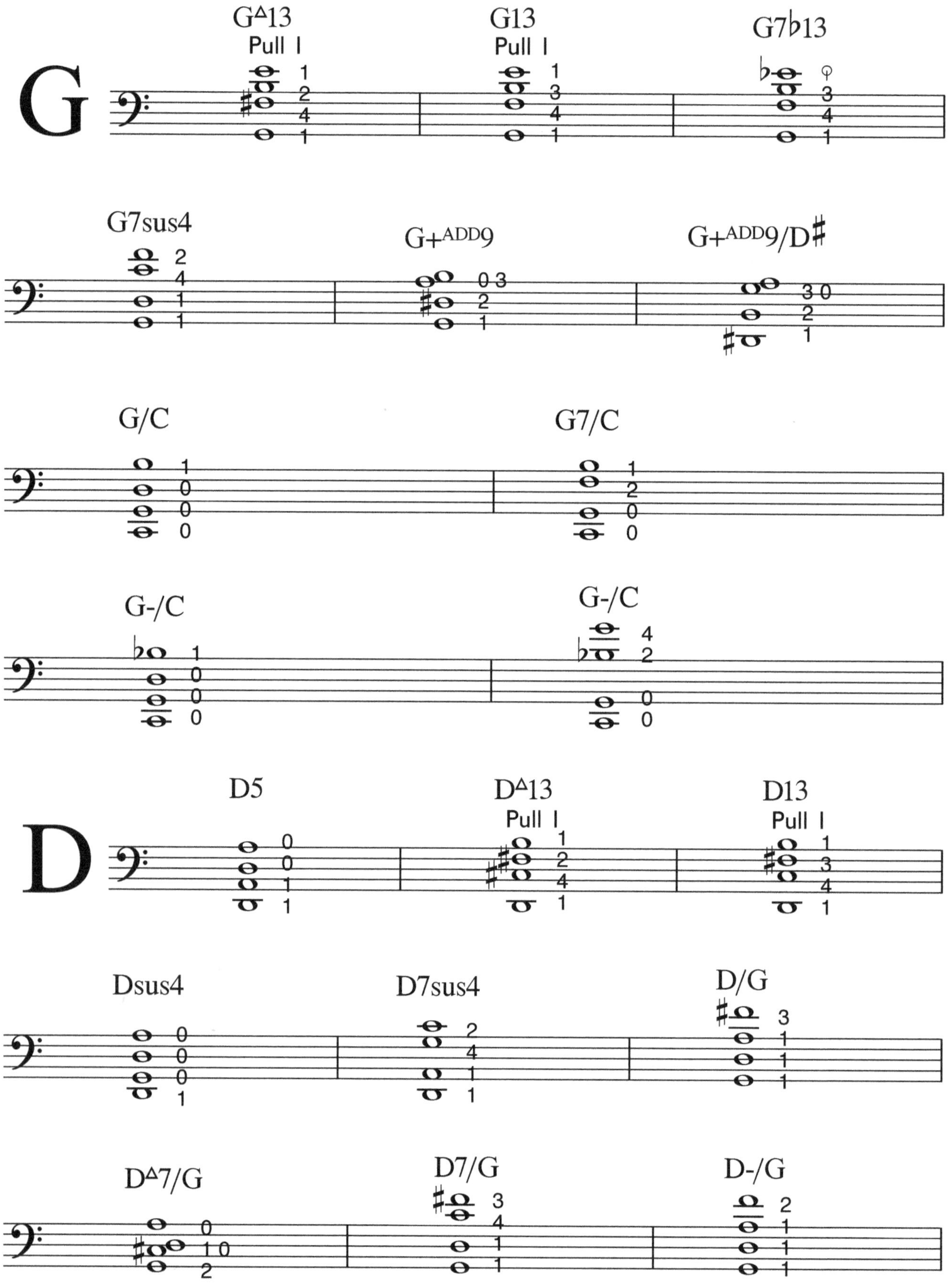
G
GΔ13
Pull I
G13
Pull I
G7♭13
G7sus4
G+ADD9
G+ADD9/D♯
G/C
G7/C
G-/C
G-/C
D
D5
DΔ13
Pull I
D13
Pull I
Dsus4
D7sus4
D/G
DΔ7/G
D7/G
D-/G

A

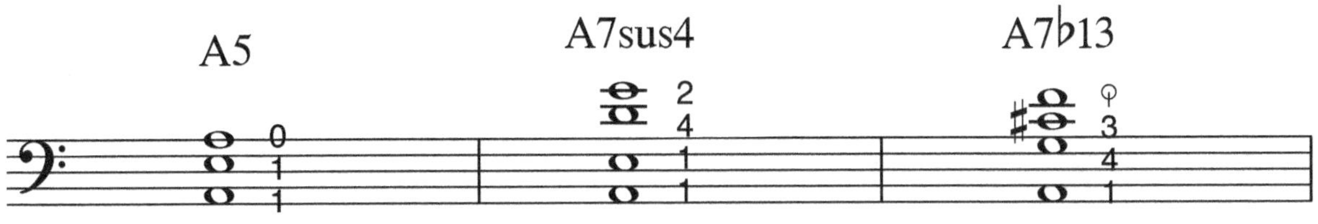
A5
A7sus4
A7♭13

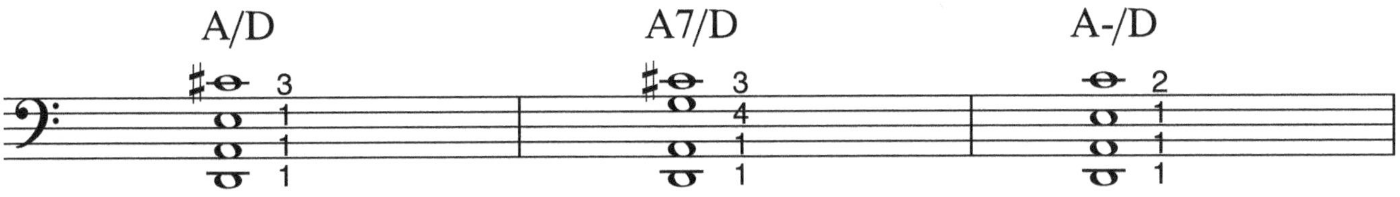
A/D
A7/D
A-/D

E

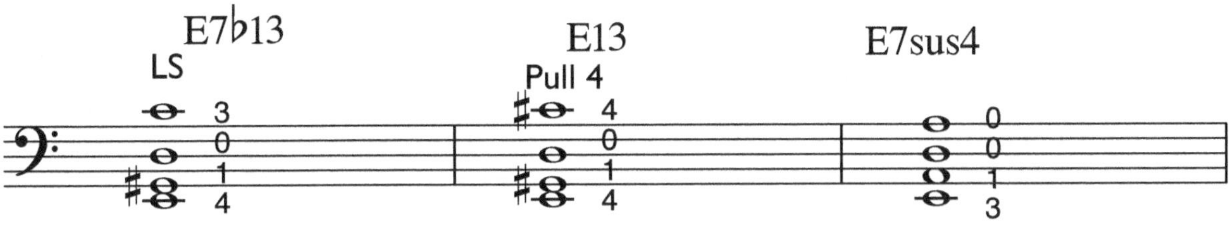
E7♭13
LS
E13
Pull 4
E7sus4

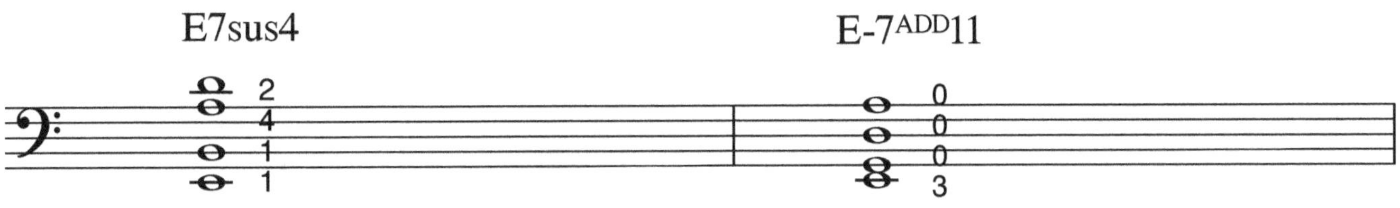
E7sus4
E-7ADD11

B

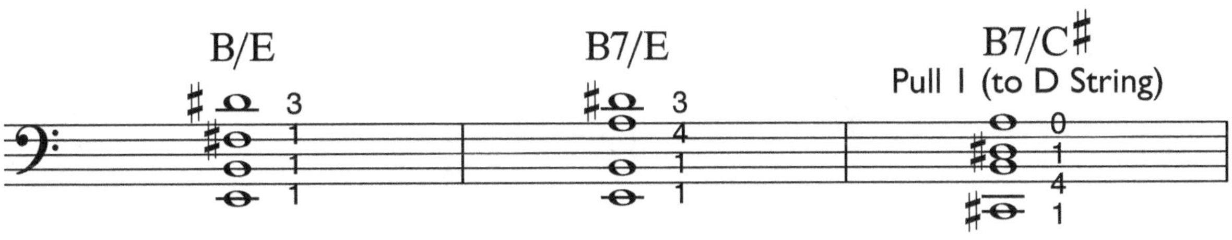
B/E
B7/E
B7/C♯
Pull 1 (to D String)

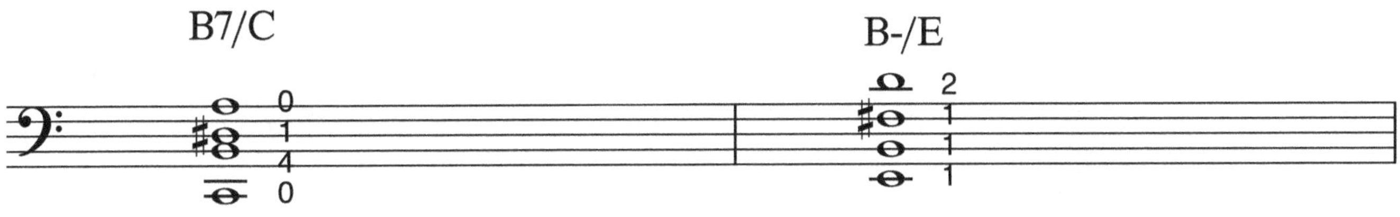
B7/C
B-/E

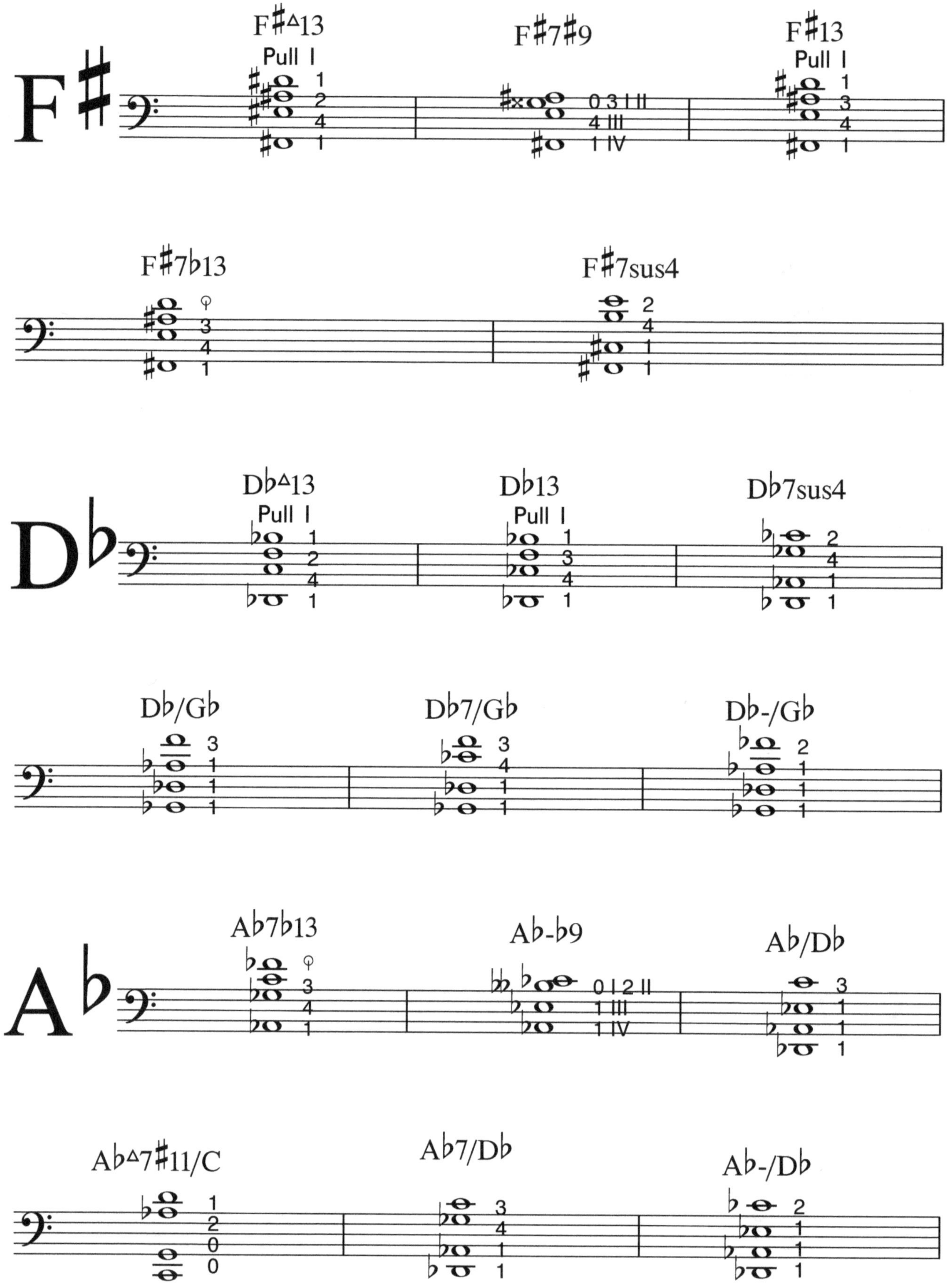
F♯
F♯△13
Pull I
F♯7♯9
F♯13
Pull I
F♯7♭13
F♯7sus4
D♭
D♭△13
Pull I
D♭13
Pull I
D♭7sus4
D♭/G♭
D♭7/G♭
D♭-/G♭
A♭
A♭7♭13
A♭-♭9
A♭/D♭
A♭△7♯11/C
A♭7/D♭
A♭-/D♭

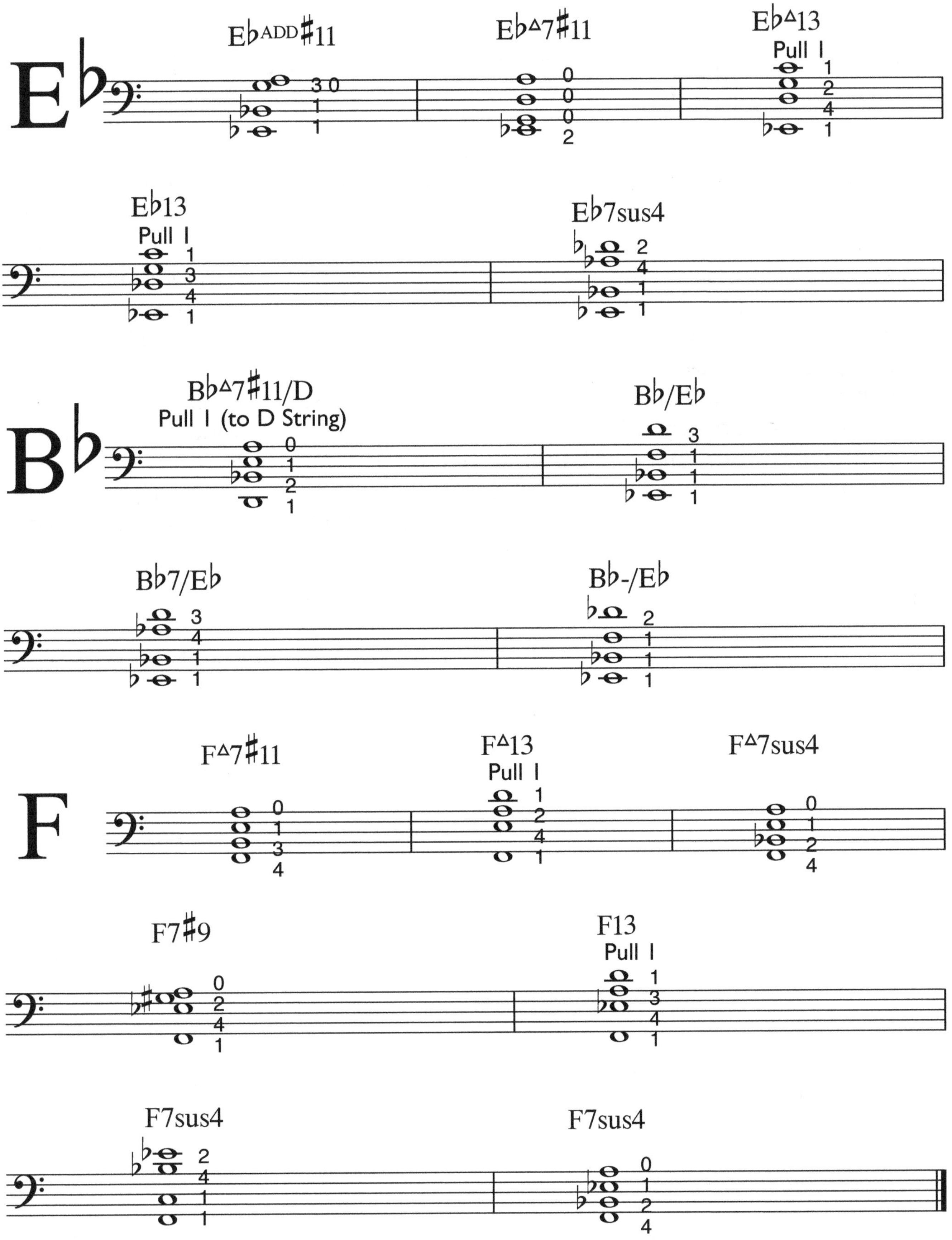
E♭
E♭ADD♯11
E♭△7♯11
E♭△13
Pull I
E♭13
Pull I
E♭7sus4
B♭
B♭△7♯11/D
Pull I (to D String)
B♭/E♭
B♭7/E♭
B♭-/E♭
F
F△7♯11
F△13
Pull I
F△7sus4
F7♯9
F13
Pull I
F7sus4
F7sus4

About the Author

Bryan Wilson is a cellist, composer, and comedian from Teaneck, New Jersey. A graduate of the California Institute of the Arts with a Bachelor of Fine Arts in Cello Performance and Music Composition, his education allowed him to create a unique voice as a cellist, composer, and comedian. As a composer, Bryan draws upon many influences, including classical, hip-hop, rock, jazz, techno, pop, and improvisation. His compositions often feature the cello singing soulful melodies over roaring synthesizers and hard-hitting drumbeats. As a cellist, Bryan has experience playing and improvising in a variety of musical situations, everything from Joseph Haydn to Bulgarian funk music. As a comedian, Bryan writes and performs funny songs with his cello at comedy clubs. He has performed his act around New York City and Los Angeles. For more information on the author, visit his website at www.bryanwilsoncello.com.